WESTON COLLEGE

B92237

D1765452

Weston College Group

Tel: 01934 411493   Email: library@weston.ac.uk

Twitter: '@wclibraryplus'

TXT 2 RENEW: 07860 023339

WITHDRAWN

Andrew Hodson

Wayfinding Design

IN THE PUBLIC ENVIRONMENT

images
Publishing

Published in Australia in 2015 by
The Images Publishing Group Pty Ltd
ABN 89 059 734 431
6 Bastow Place, Mulgrave, Victoria 3170, Australia
Tel: +61 3 9561 5544 Fax: +61 3 9561 4860
books@imagespublishing.com
www.imagespublishing.com

Copyright © The Images Publishing Group Pty Ltd 2015
The Images Publishing Group Reference Number: 1189

All rights reserved. Apart from any fair dealing for the purposes of private study,
research, criticism or review as permitted under the Copyright Act, no part of
this publication may be reproduced, stored in a retrieval system or transmitted
in any form by any means, electronic, mechanical, photocopying, recording or
otherwise, without the written permission of the publisher.

National Library of Australia Cataloguing-in-Publication entry:

Title: Wayfinding Design in the Public Environment / Andrew Hodson (ed.).
ISBN: 9781864706338 (hardback)
Subjects: Visual communication
            Signs and signboards–Design.
            Public spaces–Design.
            Graphic arts.

Dewey Number: 741.6

Coordinated and edited by Images Publishing, Shanghai office.

Printed by Toppan Leefung Printing (Shenzhen) Co. Ltd

IMAGES has included on its website a page for special notices in relation to this
and our other publications. Please visit www.imagespublishing.com.

Every effort has been made to trace the original source of copyright material
contained in this book. The publishers would be pleased to hear from copyright
holders to rectify any errors or omissions.
The information and illustrations in this publication have been prepared and
supplied by the contributor/s. While all reasonable efforts have been made
to ensure accuracy, the publishers do not, under any circumstances, accept
responsibility for errors, omissions and representations, express or implied.

INTRODUCTION

Wayfinding Design in the Public Environment has been put together to showcase some innovative and eye-catching examples of wayfinding systems in action, from internal directories through to larger scale outdoor applications. Some of the initial drawings and artworks are depicted, along with the finished projects, all of which are truly inspirational as wayfinding schemes that not only do their job, but also help to create pleasing environments, in tune with their surroundings.

Case studies within the book include hotels, shopping centers, public and corporate buildings as far afield as Brazil, Finland and Australia and show just how far the designers have gone to integrate functionality with aesthetic qualities. I am pleased to say that it also includes an example of one of ICON's projects, a temporary public wayfinding system put in place for the 2014 FIFA World Cup in Brazil, and focusing on routes to and from Rio de Janeiro's Maracanã Stadium, and around the city itself.

The increasing complexity of our public environments increasingly demands an easy-to-understand orientation and secure wayfinding that have been planned and developed by properly trained and experienced specialists. Extensive research consistently shows that the success of any public area is reliant on both thoughtful architectural and methodical wayfinding design, and it is essential that wayfinding is considered as an integral part of the architectural design process.

Wayfinding is not just about directional signage. A clear understanding of how people react in unfamiliar and complex environments, coupled with the effective use of urban, building, interior, process and information design disciplines will help create areas which are intuitive to use and easy to navigate. Signage must not be relied upon to overcome basic venue / building design inadequacies, and the requirement should be considered at an early stage of the design, following the key principles of simplicity, appropriateness and consistency of messaging style.

An effective wayfinding system has to incorporate a high level of versatility and is, at the end of the day, one of the most important means of getting residents and visitors alike around a city or venue. Aside from its directional role it can also play an important part in communicating information about events, landmarks and places of interest. Take for example the Legible London scheme, which was introduced by Transport for London (TfL) to provide an simple-to-use signage system presenting information in a range of ways to help people find their way easily and safely. Legible London is already working successfully across London, with more than 1,300 signs – half in central London and in nearly every London borough – with research showing that nine out of ten people were keen to see more Legible London signs introduced.

TfL is now working with boroughs, Business Improvement Districts and other organisations to expand the scheme further.

Any orientation system has to reflect that it is going to be used by groups with varying degrees of knowledge of a location. These can be summarised as follows:
a) Thematic routes can provide a comprehensive overview of special features and provide new visitors with a safe orientation process.
b) General plans can provide these and additional information, which may be new to the visitor, so they can find the places they knew.

So what are the main considerations for those designing a wayfinding system?
- Instantly understandable information: use simple, recognisable pictograms not only across the wayfinding elements, but also consistently throughout other informational media
- Contrasting colours and anti-glare materials
- Easy-to-read fonts and font sizes
- A simple-to-process information hierarchy from start to finish
- An easily expandable / updateable system
- Use of information points at key areas of visitor concentration, as well as pedestrian intersections or sites of special importance; especially points of arrival such as car parks, bus / train stations and airports

Finally, the onset of a wealth of digital media opens up exciting new opportunities, such as multi-lingual information, but this must be simple to use, even for those not familiar with computers. Route maps to all local amenities, attractions and facilities can be generated from the visitor's starting point, and the recent developments in smart phone technology such as QR codes, NFC (Near Field Communication) and navigation apps can provide useful and interesting additional information.

We hope you will see the importance of these elements through the case studies that follow and come to understand just how creative and artistic wayfinding can be without losing its functionality and legibility. The customer experience – be it at a one-off event, or their regular journey through the working environment – is an important consideration for the host and one which is influenced to no small extent by the wayfinding and information systems that visitors and residents encounter on a day to day basis.

Andrew Hodson

CONTENTS

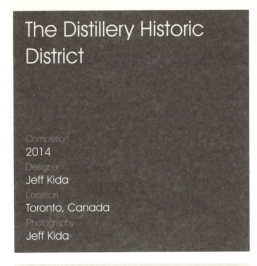

The Distillery Historic District

Completion
2014
Designer
Jeff Kida
Location
Toronto, Canada
Photography
Jeff Kida

THE DISTILLERY
HISTORIC DISTRICT

The Distillery District is a historic landmark located in the east end of Downtown Toronto, Canada. It was founded in 1832 and has recently transformed into a pedestrian-oriented area containing Café, restaurants, and shops. Jeff's concept behind this wayfinding system was to inject a fresh modern vibe into the historic precinct. The contrast is evident yet unobtrusive and seamless within the surrounding environment. With multiple entrances to this area, orientation becomes a point of emphasis. It is important that the wayfinding system helps guide or provides suggestions for pedestrians to their desired location.

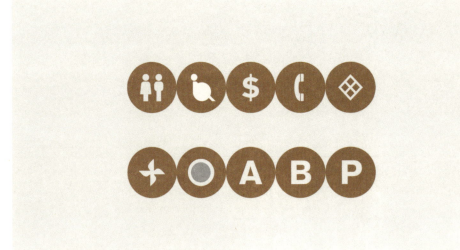

THE DISTILLERY HISTORIC DISTRICT	REGULAR
THE DISTILLERY HISTORIC DISTRICT	MEDIUM
THE DISTILLERY HISTORIC DISTRICT	**BOLD**

GRISTMILL LANE
DISTILLERY LANE
TANK HOUSE LANE
CASE GOODS LANE
PURE SPIRITS MEWS
BLACK HOUSE MEWS

TANK HOUSE LANE

← YOUNG CENTRE FOR THE PERFORMING ARTS

← BARGO DESIGNS
THE BLUE DOT GALLERY
THE BOILER HOUSE RESTAURANT
CORKIN GALLERY
DISTILL
HORSEFEATHERS HOME
AT THE DISTILLERY
JACOB GRINBERG PHOTOGRAPHY
KODIAK PHOTOGRAPHY
MILL STREET BREWPUB & STORE
PURE SPIRITS OYSTER HOUSE & GRILL
SOMA CHOCOLATE & GELATO
THE SWEET ESCAPE PATISSERIE

THE DISTILLERY HISTORIC DISTRICT

→ P →

ENTRANCE PARKING

DISTILLERY ART MARKET

MAKE YOUR WEEKEND HISTORIC

BARREL

OF FUN

WEEKEND OUTDOOR EXHIBITIONS

APRIL 15 TO OCTOBER 16, 2014

FRIDAY TO SUNDAY: 11AM - 6PM

INCLUDING MONDAYS OF

LONG WEEKENDS

THE DISTILLERY HISTORIC DISTRICT

55 MILL STREET, TORONTO, ONT

ARTSCAPE
DISTILLERY STUDIOS

THE DISTILLERY
HISTORIC DISTRICT

Wayfinding System for RIO MALL

Completion
2014
Design Agency
The Bakery design studio
Client
RIO Leninskii Mall
Location
Moscow, Russia
Photography
Lena Tsibizova

The task was very complicated. Interior design of the mall was a bit uninspiring, due to cheap materials and excessive lighting. After repositioning the Mall to cater to a more demanding audience, the wayfinding system had to be contemporary and sophisticated. The designers based the design around the name Rio. Using wood and moss, they tried to bring a Brasilian forest vibe to the space and make the interior friendly and fun.

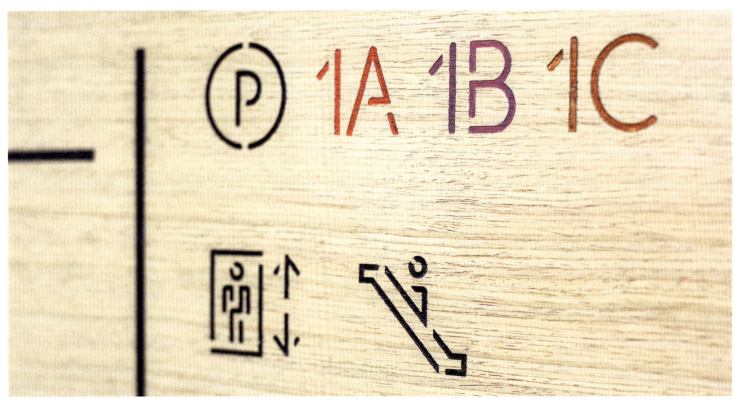

Ainoa

Completion year
2014
Design Agency
Bond Creative Agency
Designer
Marko Salonen
Client
Ainoa
Location
Espoo, Finland
Photography
Angel Gil

Ainoa is a shopping centre in garden city Tapiola, located in the western part of Greater Helsinki. Bond was asked to create a visual identity and a graphic design for the interior. The coherent language flows throughout the shopping centre, including logo, illustrations, icons and arrows.

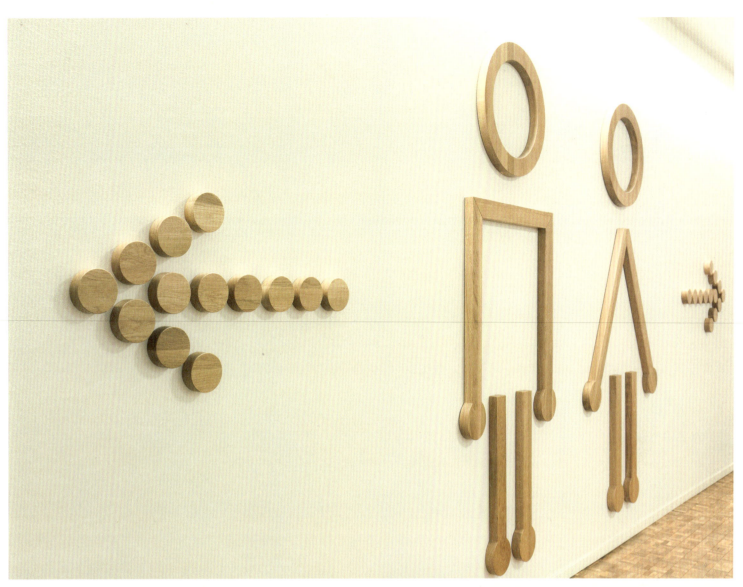

The designers' idea was to bring garden idea to design language with very minimal style and follow that with discipline. For the same reason the architecture company wanted to use real wood as much as possible and they decided to cut graphics to wooden surfaces. Their target was to stand out from regular shopping centres with solutions which stand the test of time.

Cine Theatro Brasil

Completion
2014
Design Agency
Greco Design
Client
Associação V&M do Brasil
Location
Belo Horizonte, Brazil
Photography
Rafael Motta

This project is about the redesign of the Cine Theatro Brasil's façade and wayfinding system. Being one of the country's first movie theatre, it was integrated back into the city after 15 years of being abandoned and was returned to the population in a restoration quest that preserved the outlines and architecture of the theater's original era. The façade project uses typography as a means to recover the identity of one of Brazil's oldest movie theaters. Inspired by the singularity of its original façade sign, a study of its typographical elements was done. The inner signage design sought to enhance the theater's original architectural features. Details of the façade and stairways' ironworks were the inspiration for creating artdecographisms used for designing the equipment and the totems' structure.

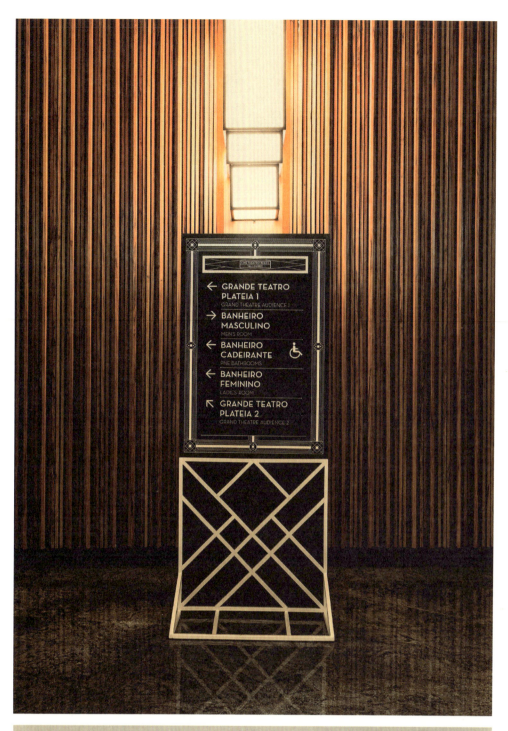

Stejarii Country Club Parking

Completion
2013
Designers
Daniel&Andrew, Diseñate
Location
Bucharest, Romania
Photography
Cosmin Dragomir

Stejarii Country Club is a new sports and wellness facility located near Băneasa forest, outside of Bucharest. Daniel & Andrew developed the environmental graphics and wayfindings of the facility's underground parking.

The graphic design expresses motion and is centred on the dynamic portrayal of the sports you can practice in the facility and the motivational text messages. The bold colours are associated with the sport scenes but help you easily find your parking space. The graphic design of the parking is essential because it represents the first impression the facility leaves on its clients.

Multispace Signage Concept

Completion	Client
2014	**Swiss Federal Railways SBB**
Design Agency	
Büro4	Location
Designers	**Switzerland**
Dominik Wullschleger,	Photography
Stefan Hunziker,	**Markus Bertschi**
Lukas Wanner	

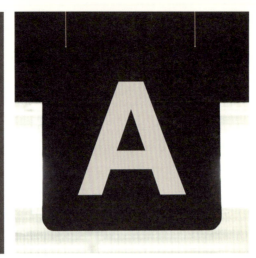

Ausrichtung der Schilder auf Oberkante 167cm

Ausrichtung der Schilder auf Oberkante 150cm

A generic orientation concept for open-plan offices is based on the functional and formal criteria of Swiss railway station signage and meeting SBB's high design standards.

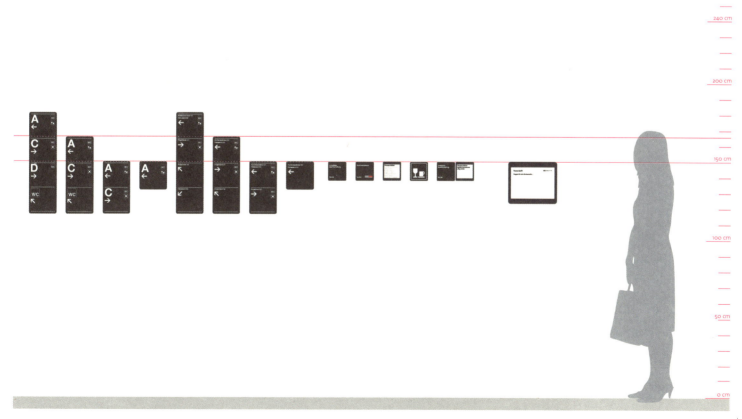

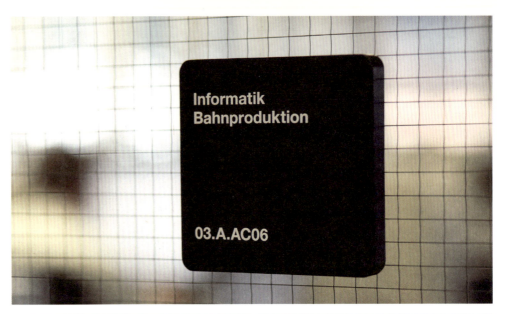

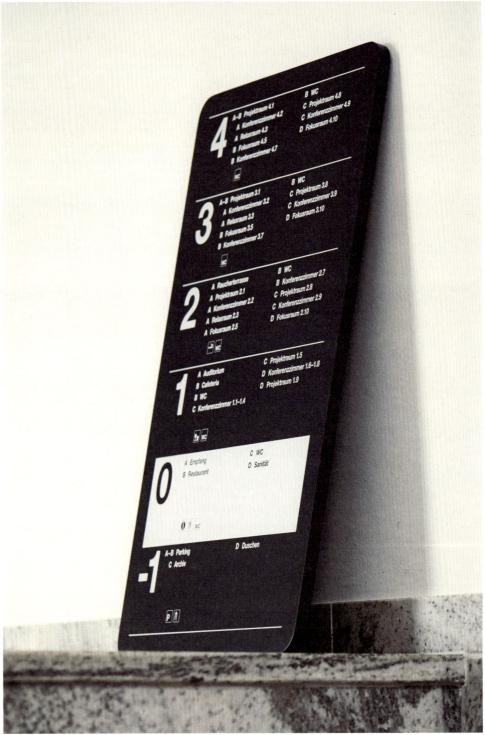

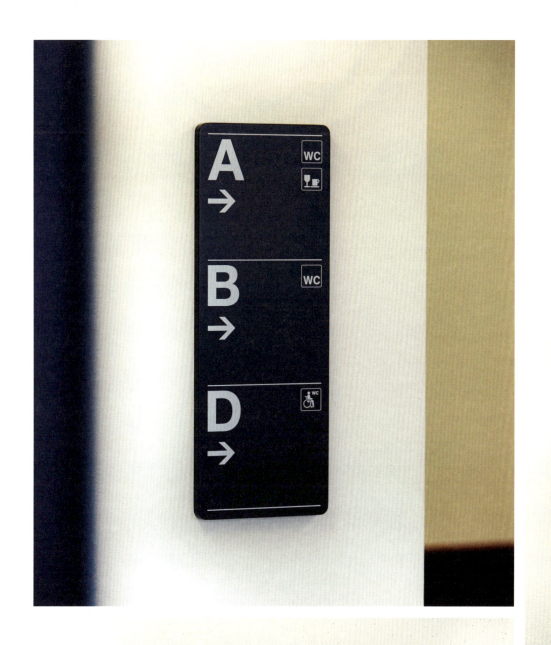

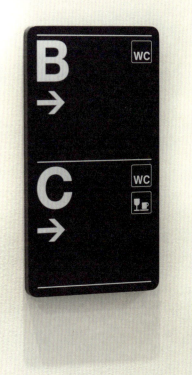

Kö-Bogen Düsseldorf

Completion
2014
Design Agency
Nowakteufelknyrim
Designers
Stefan Nowak, Dominik Mycielski, Tobias Jochinke
Client
Zechbau
Location
Dusseldorf , Germany
Photography
Stefan Nowak

In collaboration with Studio Daniel Libeskind, an orientation system was developed that evolved from the design language and the materials of the building out. Great emphasis was placed on the continuity of information services – overview, guidance and navigation. All materials and structural elements are designed for long-lasting performance; they are also easy to clean and maintain. A convincing and appropriate solution includes the integration of projected information (GOBO light technology) in the complex architecture of the individual foyers. The steles in the outdoor area are also designed for future integration of electronic media.

Königsallee 2a

+3
Breuninger
Verwaltung

+1
Sansibar

0
Ausgang

-2 -3
Parkebenen

.4

Ausgang

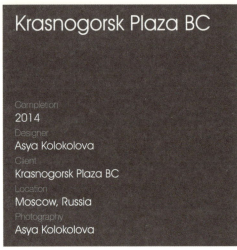

Krasnogorsk Plaza BC

Completion
2014
Designer
Asya Kolokolova
Client
Krasnogorsk Plaza BC
Location
Moscow, Russia
Photography
Asya Kolokolova

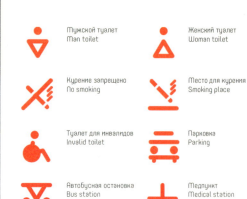

Мужской туалет / Man toilet	Женский туалет / Woman toilet
Курение запрещено / No smoking	Место для курения / Smoking place
Туалет для инвалидов / Invalid toilet	Парковка / Parking
Автобусная остановка / Bus station	Медпункт / Medical station

The logo is simple. This design is based on the direct association with the name of the business centre (name of the town Krasnogorsk translates approximately into English as Red Hills). Also, on the emblem of Krasnogorsk town there are 3 red hills. That was displayed in the logo.

Designed logo became foundation for the navigation system. Red Hills transformed into the arrows which rotate around the centre point. And based on the simple lines of the logo have been developed essential icons.

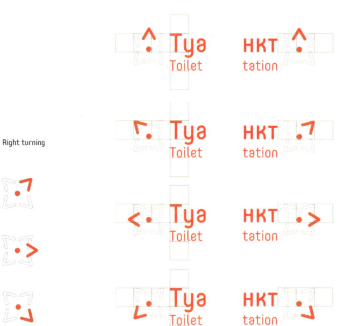

Base	Left turning	Up/down/ location	Right turning

Source point			

08 Офисы 801 • 870
Вертолётная площадка

07 Офисы 701 • 799

06 Офисы 601 • 699

05 Офисы 501 • 599

04 Офисы 401 • 499

03 Офисы 301 • 399
Администрация

02 Офисы 201 • 299   Фитнес-клуб
Магазины   Салон красоты
Кафе

01 Офисы 101 • 150
Бюро пропусков
Кафе

00 Парковка
Супермаркет

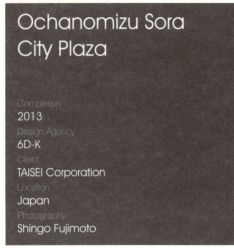

Ochanomizu Sora City Plaza

Completion
2013
Design Agency
6D-K
Client
TAISEI Corporation
Location
Japan
Photography
Shingo Fujimoto

This project is a VI (Visual Identity) and sign plan of the office building, which is located in front of the station in Tokyo Ochanomizu. Usually office building may not set VI because there is the replacement of various companies. However, a lot of similar buildings are built in this area, making it hard to find the underground entrance, over ground entrance, etc. Since it is difficult for people to figure out their position, the designer produced VI and decided to design the Sign centering on VI. This area is called "Ochanomizu", meaning a clean water place. It is expressed in the name of "Soracity" concept to the building.

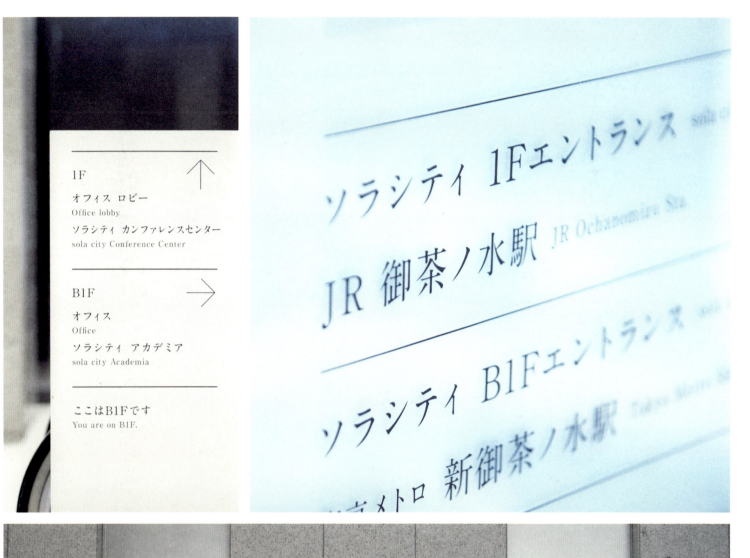

1F	↑
オフィス ロビー Office lobby ソラシティ カンファレンスセンター sola city Conference Center	
B1F	→
オフィス Office ソラシティ アカデミア sola city Academia	

ここはB1Fです
You are on B1F.

ソラシティ 1Fエントランス sola ci

JR 御茶ノ水駅 JR Ochanomizu Sta

ソラシティ B1Fエントランス sol

東京メトロ 新御茶ノ水駅 Tokyo Metro Sh

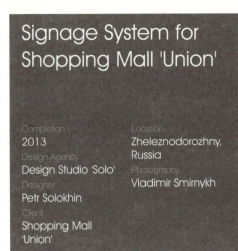

Signage System for Shopping Mall 'Union'

Completion
2013
Design Agency
Design Studio 'Solo'
Designer
Petr Solokhin
Client
Shopping Mall 'Union'

Location
Zheleznodorozhny, Russia
Photography
Vladimir Smirnykh

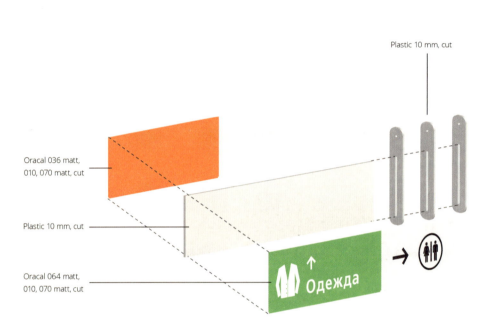

Plastic 10 mm, cut

Oracal 036 matt, 010, 070 matt, cut

Plastic 10 mm, cut

Oracal 064 matt, 010, 070 matt, cut

Design Studio 'Solo' developed and installed signage system for a 3-storeyed shopping mall in the Moscow region.

Taking into account architectural peculiarities of the shopping mall, the designer developed a neat and clear signage system.

The ease of the production and installation of the signs allowed to cut the costs for these phases considerably. To do this, the design of the sighs was developed so that there was little hand work required and the number of parts was minimal.

As a result, the studio prepared the drawings according to which the milling machine did all the job and the installation team only had to deal with the signs as with an erector set and put them in the shopping mall.

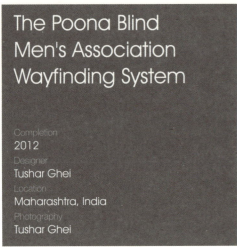

The Poona Blind Men's Association Wayfinding System

Completion
2012
Designer
Tushar Ghei
Location
Maharashtra, India
Photography
Tushar Ghei

The brief here was to create a family of sign types that not only addressed primary information and wayfinding needs but also recognised secondary issues and audiences with an appropriate information hierarchy.

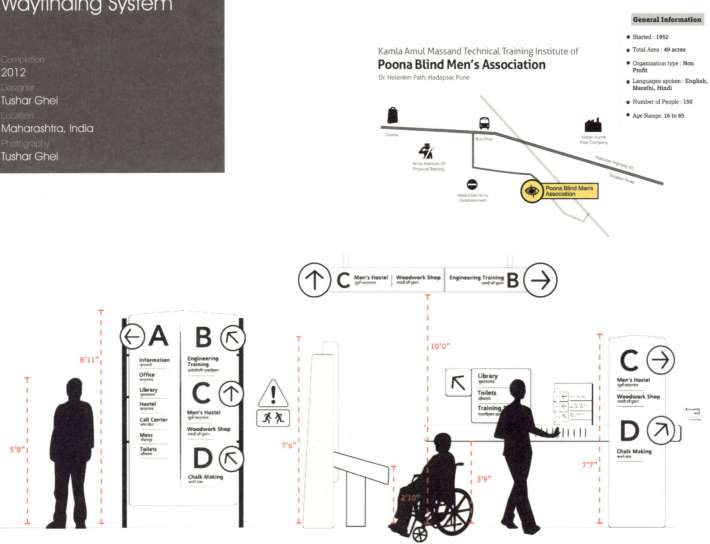

Kamla Amul Massand Technical Training Institute of
Poona Blind Men's Association
Dr. Helenker Path, Hadapsar, Pune

General Information

- Started : 1952
- Total Area : 49 acres
- Organization type : Non Profit
- Languages spoken : English, Marathi, Hindi
- Number of People : 150
- Age Range : 16 to 65

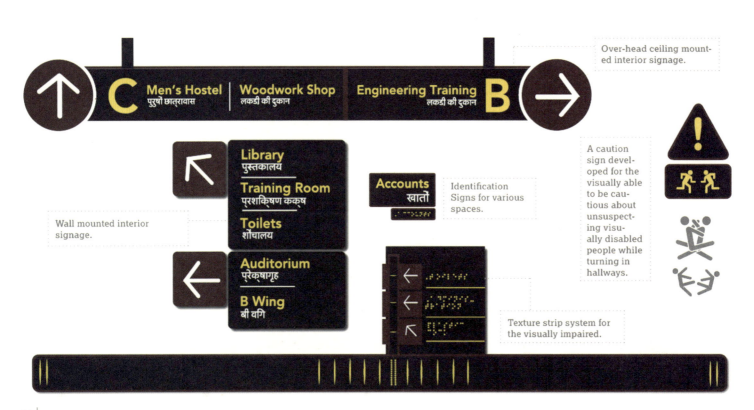

Over-head ceiling mounted interior signage.

A caution sign developed for the visually able to be cautious about unsuspecting visually disabled people while turning in hallways.

Identification Signs for various spaces.

Wall mounted interior signage.

Texture strip system for the visually impaired.

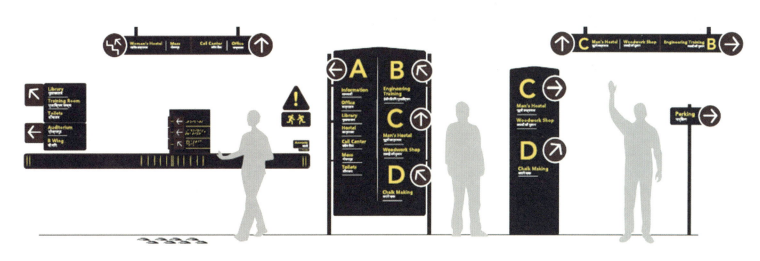

Exterior Signage

A welcome sign which will be placed at the entrance of the main building with general information about the facility with a *tactile map*.

Elevated dots of *'Tacdots'* are placed before all freestanding signs to alert the visually impaired about an obsticle. The tacdots produce a specific sound when the struck with a cane.

The main free standing sign which will be erected before the entry point outside the gate.

Free standing signs wchich will be placed between building B and A where there is no walking path.

The parking sign which will be placed at the entry point.

Kangan Institute Wayfinding

Completion
2013
Designer
Another Matt Ryan
Client
Kangan Institute, Automotive Centre of Excellence
Location
Melbourne Docklands, Australia
Photography
Mark Duffus

The wayfinding package was implemented across an existing building, and showcased the newly constructed stage 2 "feature" building with the potential for a third stage in the near future.

Complimenting the Institute's world leading automotive training facilities, a unique wayfinding methodology was conceptualised that no longer relied upon traditional navigational aids and user responses.

This approach focuses on the user's immediate surroundings, not their ability to orientate themselves to an imaginary North Point to gain an understanding of where they are within the building.

Using this Relative Room Positioning (RRP©) system, only relevant information (based on the users location, immediate surroundings and intended destination) is provided, significantly reducing the amount of information the user must process and recall. This greatly reduces the amount of information and therefore any intimidation usually associated with the confronting amount of visual clutter.

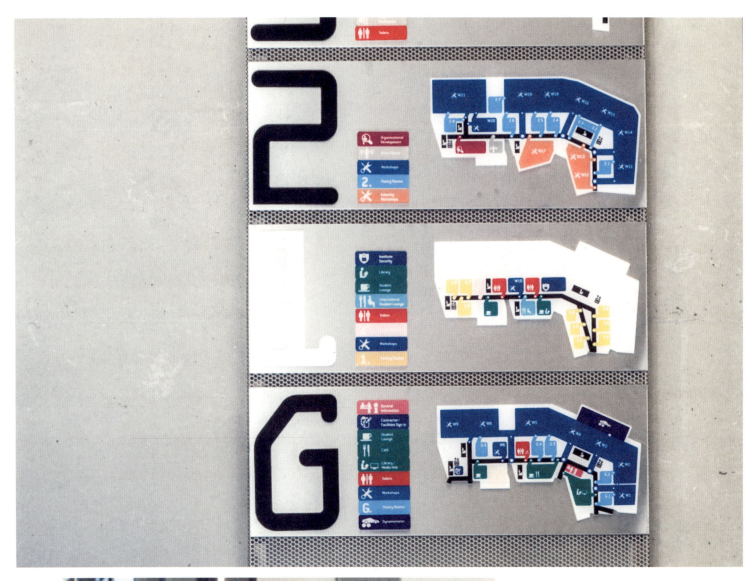

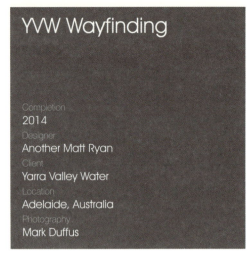

YVW Wayfinding

Completion
2014
Designer
Another Matt Ryan
Client
Yarra Valley Water
Location
Adelaide, Australia
Photography
Mark Duffus

The design responded to essential service Yarra Valley Water provides to the community, the supply of fresh clean water. The design concept was inspired by the movement and vast array of colours evident as light refracts through water, revealing its beautiful colour spectrum.

To simplify the design over so many buildings, individual branding iconography using unique colour palettes was developed for each building on site.

The calculated use of colour within the building's branding, iconography and environmental graphics was a key reference for the user's navigation throughout the buildings as many were in fact joined in areas. The problem of distinguishing areas without having to display additional levels of information, was solved which therefore reducd the number of signs and directional aids required.

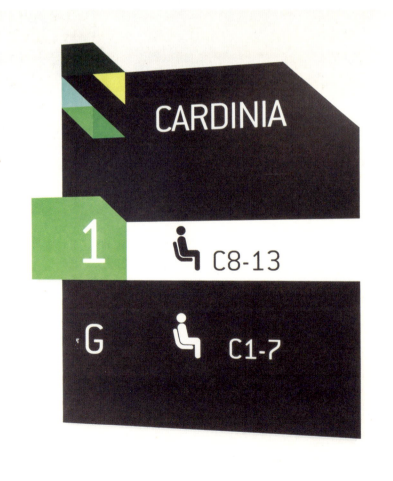

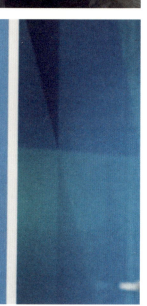

Precinct 75 Site Signage

Completion
2014

Location
NSW, Australia

Designers
Dari Israelstam,
Anthony Smith,
Bonnie Nguyen

Photography
Courtesy of
Precinct 75

Client
Precinct 75 (JVM
Holdings & Chalak
Holdings Pty Ltd)

Universal Favourite designed the identity and wayfinding for the Precinct 75 site.

It is perfectly positioned in south Sydney's growing creative business community of St Peters. It has a rich heritage dating back to the early 1900s. The character of the original site has been maintained, offering the period charm of high ceilings, exposing timber and raw finishes.

The invigorated identity system brings a fresh and contemporary flavour to refocus Precinct 75 as an important creative hub.

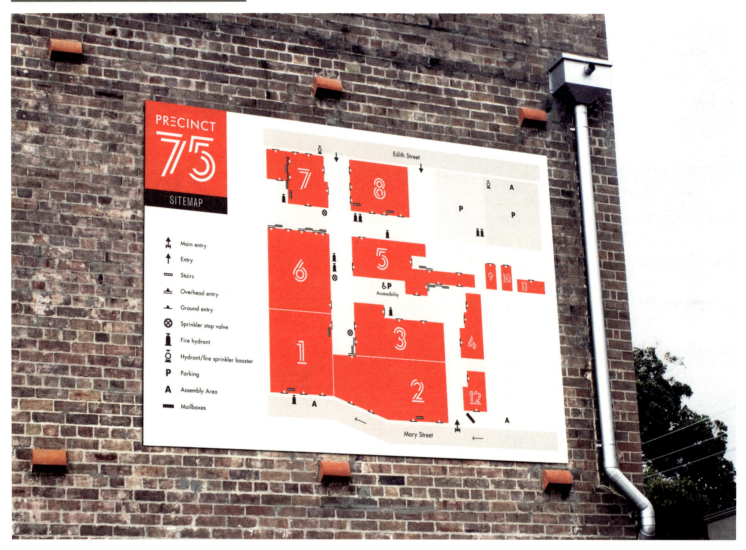

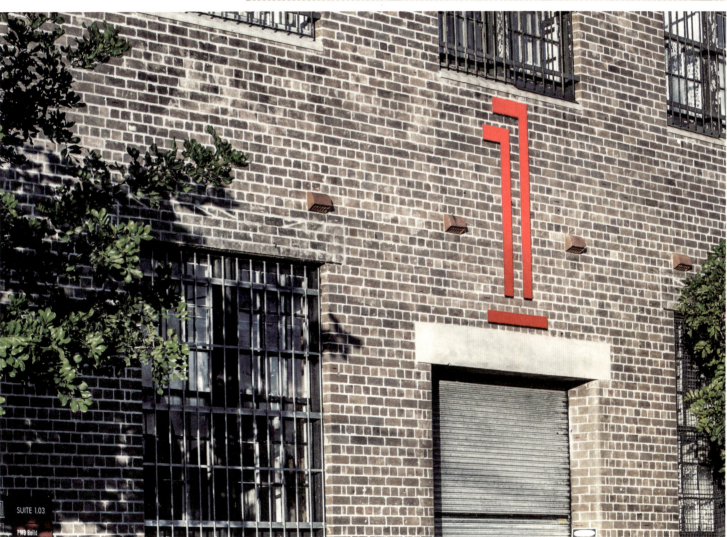

Wayfinding included signage for the site's main entrances, building numbers and individual suites as well as the site directories.

BL Stream Office

Completion
2013

Design Agency
Medusagroup, Kolektyf

Designers
Pawel Ceglowski, Bartosz Kedzierski, Konrad Iwanowski, Marek Jozefczuk

Client
BL Stream

Location
Wrocław, Poland

Photography
Karolina Kosowicz

Kolektyf was chosen by BL Stream to design and execute graphic design for their HQ in Wroclaw. BL Stream is an international IT business offering a wide range of web and mobile solutions.

Their inspiration for this project was the design of mobile phone operating systems (IOS7 and Windows Phone 8) for which BL Systems deigned applications. The main feature was based on Windows 8 famous tiles and corporate colors of BL Stream. This was balanced by white lettering, iconography and signage.

Kolektyf designed the wayfinding system for the reception and lounge area, the corridors, conference rooms, kitchen, playroom and design room. They have also managed to graphically present the timeline of the company history and its achievements.

Green Day Office Building

Completion
2013

Client
Skanska

Design Agency
Medusagroup,
Kolektyf

Location
Wroclaw, Poland

Photography
Bartosz Holoszkiewicz

Designers
Przemo Lukasik,
Lukasz Zagala,
Joanna Sowula,
Konrad Iwanowski,
Bartosz Kedzierski,
Bartosz Zielinski.

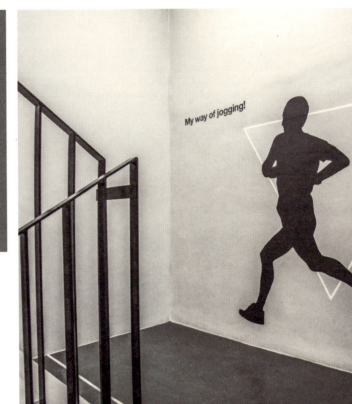

This project encompasses graphics and wayfinding for communal spaces and outside signage of the whole building as well. It also includes graphic design for a client occupying 6 floors. Every floor for this building has been given its own geometric figure and colour.

Communal spaces have been kept as neutral as possible by using minimal amount of colour, whereas colours are more visible in open spaces and bathrooms.

Green Towers Office Building

Completion
2013
Design Agency
Medusagroup,
Kolektyf
Designers
Przemo Lukasik,
Lukasz Zagala,
Joanna Sowula,
Wojciech Eksner

Konrad Iwanowski,
Bartosz Kedzierski,
Bartosz Zielinski.
Client
Skanska
Location
Lodz, Poland
Photography
Bartosz Holoszkiewicz

Bespoke graphic for wayfinding in this building was designed by Medusagroup, however the execution was given to Kolektyf who developed the details. Green Towers is the first site in Poland that has obtained the platinum award of LEED Shell & Core.

This project not only plays a part in finding your way within the building, but also becomes an attractive graphic element which makes Green Towers very unique. This project has additional value in terms of its 'eco-factor' by visually promoting energy saving, recycling and taking the stairs.

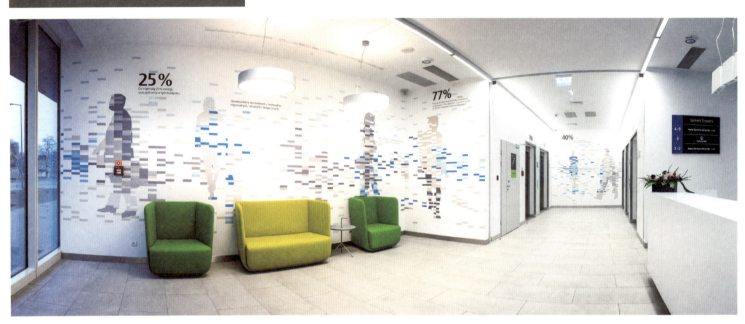

Completion
2013

Design Agency
Medusagroup,
Kolektyf

Designers
Przemo Lukasik,
Lukasz Zagala,
Joanna Sowula,
Wojciech Eksner

Konrad Iwanowski,
Bartosz Kedzierski,
Bartosz Zielinski.

Client
Skanska

Location
Lodz, Poland

Photography
Bartosz Holoszkiewicz

The graphic design of this project tells a story of a factory operating between 1924 and 2005. Today a big office block stands here and it was certified by energy saving LEED Silver.

Visual complexity of this project uses originality of historic graphics and documents illustrating the textiles factory of Ajzyk Piaskowski. Black and white designs are visible by the entrance and lift corridors, whilst colours are to identify four different entrances and a parking for the building.

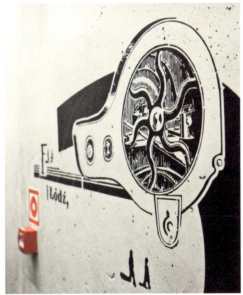

Dock10, Media City UK on Behalf of Peel Holdings

Completion
2013
Design Agency
NoChintz
Client
Dock10
Location
Salford, UK
Photography
Joel Fildes

Dock10 is one of Europe's leading digital media service providers. Programmes made in dock10's seven HD studios, two audio studios and 27 edit suites, include the Voice, Match of the Day, Blue Peter, Happy Valley and Last Tango in Halifax.

Located in Media City UK, dock10's 24,000 square meters purpose-built facility opened in 2011 and is constantly evolving in line with industry and client needs. Keen to keep it easy for clients and visitors to find their way around the vast building, dock10 appointed NoChintz to design, create and implement a simple, straightforward wayfinding system.

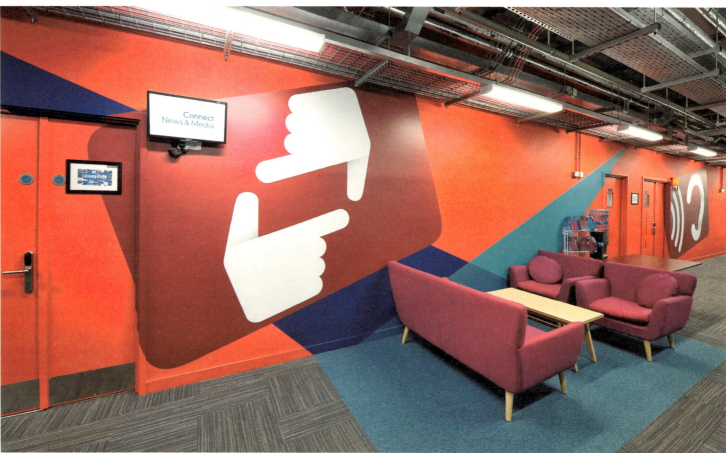

They developed a graphic system inspired by traditional media 'buttons'; pause icons to make visitors stop and orientate themselves; play arrows to point people in the right direction; and fast forward icons to indicate the need to keep moving. Destination points were allocated to demonstrate the location of a department, and information portals were created to contextualise particular parts of the building.

They also refreshed the corridors of dock10; with a combination of colour and large format bespoke icon. NoChintz Identity and Interiors worked seamlessly to complete this project and are thrilled with the outcome.

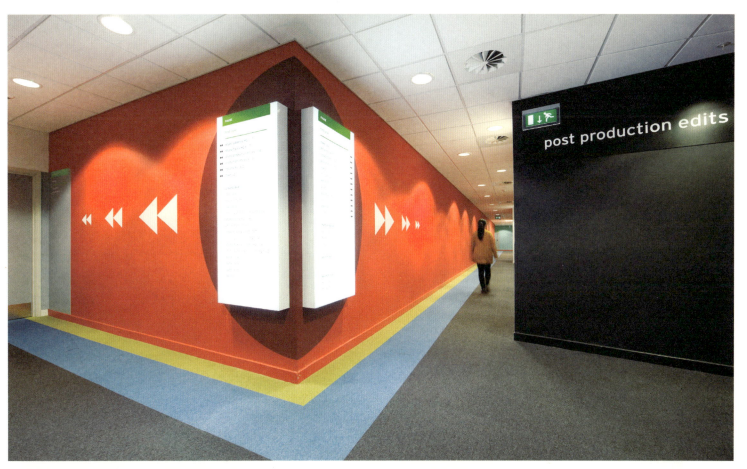

Adshel Interior

Completion
2013
Design Agency
THERE
Designers
Paul Tabouré, Jon Zhu
Client
Adshel
Location
Sydney, Australia
Photography
Steve Brown

Adshel now has a compelling brand identity that doesn't look or act like anything else in category. It's multicoloured when surrounded by grey; it can share a laugh when many are too serious; it embraces innovation where many are timid in the face of relentless change. This dynamic and flexible identity reflects the organisations of today, and helps guide them on their journey ahead.

Using their new contemporary flexible Adshel brand, THERE integrated the brand into their workplace environment. Consisting of lobby arrival graphics, branded reception desk, WOW lobby feature wall, lift lobby graphics, door signage and breakout areas THERE transformed their workspace into a space more reflective and true to their revitalised brand image. The designers added a more dynamic approach to traditional graphics through the use of bright neon illuminated signage.

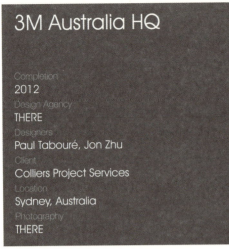

3M Australia HQ

Completion
2012
Design Agency
THERE
Designers
Paul Tabouré, Jon Zhu
Client
Colliers Project Services
Location
Sydney, Australia
Photography
THERE

The designers delivered a complete signage solution that captured the 3M brand essence 'Harnessing the chain reaction of new ideas' and celebrated the culture of innovation which is at the heart of 3M. The scope included all custom designed, internal and external identification signage, wayfinding signs, plinths and statutary.

A variety of materials and finishes were utilised with each sign fabricated from a single, folding, laser cut piece of powder coated aluminium. The company's rich heritage was further celebrated with an 80 square meters routed timeline wall relief that showcased the company's brand evolution over the last hundred years.

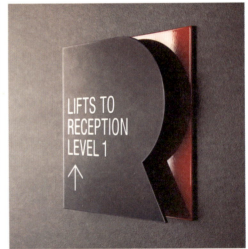

LIFTS TO RECEPTION

PASSPORT

1957 The Sydney office moves to the Leedam Branch building on Wentworth Avenue, Sydney NSW – Australia

1958 The Melbourne office relocates to 17/23 Queensbridge Street, Melbourne VIC – Australia

The Tasmanian branch opens at 201 Elizabeth Street, Hobart TAS – Australia

The South Melbourne branch opens at 8 Bond Terrace, Adelaide SA – Australia

959 The Brisbane branch opens at the Plumbridge Building at 166 Barry Parade, Brisbane QLD – Australia

Worldwide results are consolidated and sales exceed $300 million

Sustainable Industries Education Centre

Completion
2014

Design Agency
Parallax Design

Designers
Matthew Remphrey,
Andrew Smart

Client
Department of
Further Education,

**Science and
Technology**

Location
Adelaide, Australia

Photography
David Sievers

As a major tenant of the centre, TafeSA was the state's largest provider of vocational education and training. It intended to relocate all of its construction trades to SIEC. Parallax was commissioned to develop a comprehensive signage system allowing staff, students and visitors to navigate five buildings (inserted into the existing building) across four levels and open workshops – some 45,000 square meters in total.

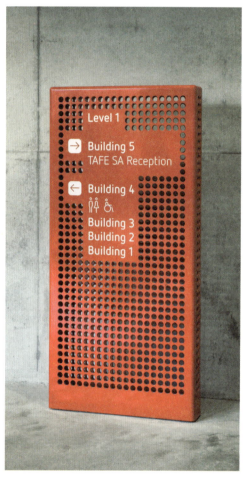

The architectural approach to refurbishing the existing building was to present it honestly, with all materials and services visible. The very building became a teaching aid. A recurring motif was the use of fins in varying sizes, spacing and materials, which produce a moire effect on the light. The designers used these fins for graphics that can be seen from one direction and hidden from another view, and perforated aluminium to create a moire pattern effect the viewers experiences when they move past, over and under the signs. The shear scale of the building was another consideration. Down the main "street" connecting entrances and bisecting buildings and workshop, they designed a series of 7 meters high perforated navigational totems. The totems are completely self-supporting with no internal structure, and possess a lightness that belies their size. They were also responsible for developing a strategy that named buildings, located rooms, indicated pedestrian and vehicular movement in the open workshops, and took into account PPE, HAZMAT and emergency signage requirements.

Signage System For Lanit office

Completion
2014

Client
Lanit it company

Design Agency
ZOLOTO group

Location
Moscow, Russia

Designer
Andrey Trukhan

Photography
Svyat Vishnakov

LANIT – one of the leading Russian IT companies – has recently moved to a new 10-storey office building which houses over 2,000 employees. At such scale interior navigation becomes complicated.

A unique visual interior navigation system developed by ZOLOTO group specially for LANIT is highly functional, which is based on the company's logo and field. Not arrows and signs but continual colour lines lead you from point to point, reminding cables of a modern building and representing the company's conception – the principal of continuity. Thus the interior assumes individuality, reason and identity of high-quality visual style.

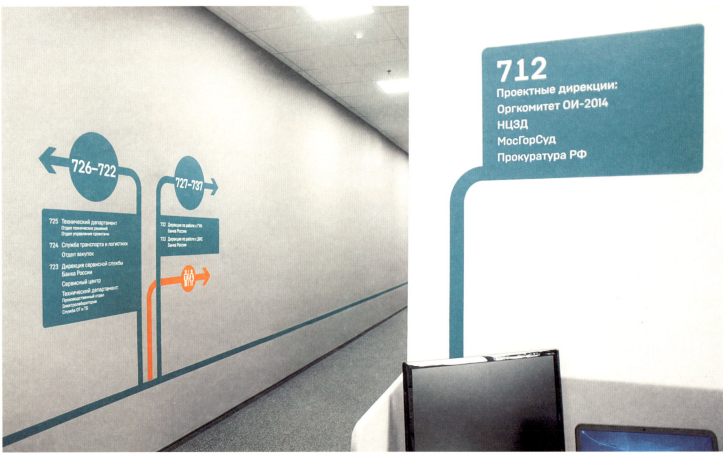

726–722

725 Технический департамент
Отдел технических решений
Отдел управления проектами

724 Служба транспорта и логистики
Отдел закупок

723 Дирекция сервисной службы
Банка России

Сервисный центр

Технический департамент:
Производственный отдел
Электролаборатория
Служба ОТ и ТБ

727–737

722 Дирекция по работе с ГУН
Банка России

733 Дирекция по работе с ДИС
Банка России

712

Проектные дирекции:
Оргкомитет ОИ–2014
НЦЗД
МосГорСуд
Прокуратура РФ

ИНСИСТЕМС

701 Проектная дирекция:
Альфа Банк / Банк Открытие

703 Департамент Энергетики

705 Проектная дирекция:
Перераспределение отделений СБ РФ
ЦСАО Перераспределение отделений СБ РФ
Сбербанк / Дочерние компании

707 Проектная дирекция:
Газпром, Роснефть

709 Бухгалтерия

712 Проектные дирекции:
Оргкомитет ОИ–2014 / НЦЗД / МосГорСуд
Прокуратура РФ

714 Дирекция строительства энергетических
объектов

716 Служба IT

Отдел рекламы и PR

Служба персонала

718 Финансовая служба

Юридическая служба

723 Дирекция сервисной службы Банка России

Сервисный центр

Технический департамент:
Производственный отдел Электролаборатория
Служба ОТ и ТБ

724 Служба транспорта и логистики

Отдел закупок

725 Технический департамент
Отдел управления проектами

732 Дирекция по работе с ГУН Банка России

733 Дирекция по работе с ДИС Банка России

RSPCA Victoria Head Office

Completion
2014

Location
Victoria, Australia

Design Agency
Crampton d+a

Photography
David Crampton

Designer
David Crampton

Client
RSPCA and Bamford-Dash architects

The new four-level centre for RSPCA accommodates administrative offices, clinical and welfare functions as well as the RSPCA's extensive pool of volunteers and a range of public facilities including a café, shop, dog spa and pet adoption facilities.

All these facilities required identification from the promotional pylon sign at street level right down to the name on the entry door to the cat adoption.

The pixilated 'tree of life' donation wall commemorates the different levels of sponsorship from companies to individuals. The different amounts are represented by different thickness of squares, the different size of the pixel of the squares and the colour of the printed names.

Zahran Business Centre Wayfinding

Completion
2014
Design Agency
Slash
Designers
Marcos Cruz,
Patricia Cansado,
Filipa Goes,
Waleed Bahadi

Client
Zahran Business
Centre
Location
Jeddah, Kingdom of
Saudi Arabia
Photography
Nuno Abreu

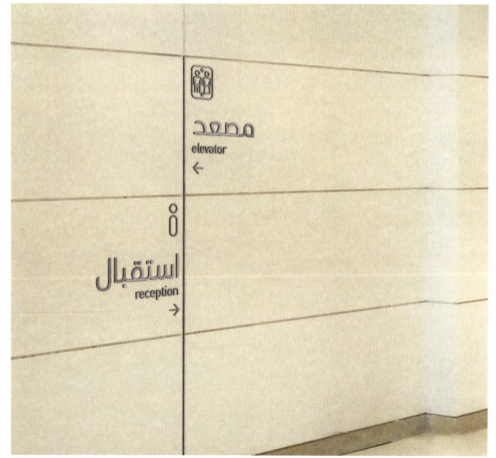

Located in a major commercial district in Jeddah, Zahran Business Centre is a state-of-the-art office and retail centre. It consists of 14 floors of commercial space towering 262.47 feet designed to represent itself as a landmark commercial facility. Our challenge was to develop and oversee the implementation of a consistent wayfinding system.

Slash was asked to develop and oversee the implementation of a consistent wayfinding system for the business centre. It involved in developing a custom series of icons, typographic arrangements and materials that related to the environment in which they would be placed in.

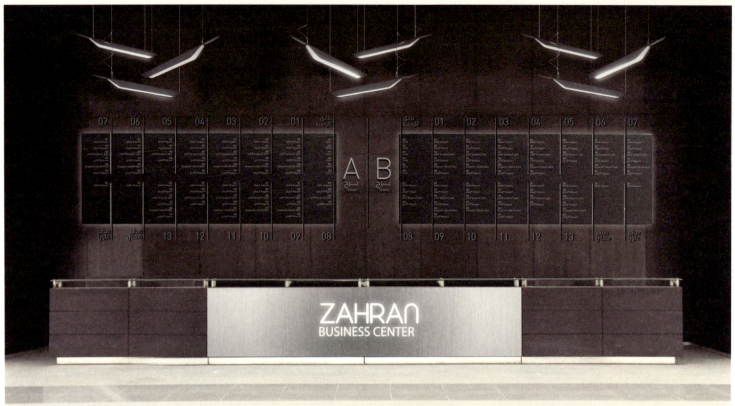

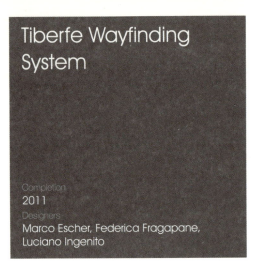

Tiberfe Wayfinding System

Completion
2011
Designers
Marco Escher, Federica Fragapane,
Luciano Ingenito

Tiberfe is a fictional Portuguese city. The corporate identity and the wayfinding system are aesthetically inspired by the traditional Portuguese iconography. Colours, textures and shapes are inspired by azulejos, the traditional Portuguese tiles. The different panels are composed of three layers: a central layer decorated with textures that recall azulejos and two external layers, whose shape (obtained from the airport logo) shows the texture inside.

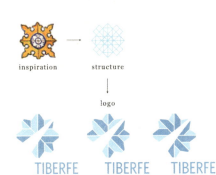

inspiration → structure

logo

TIBERFE *international airport* TIBERFE *international airport* TIBERFE *international airport*

abc

directional signage

arrivals and departures   services

abc   abc

walls

abc

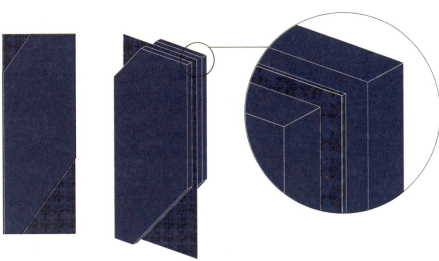

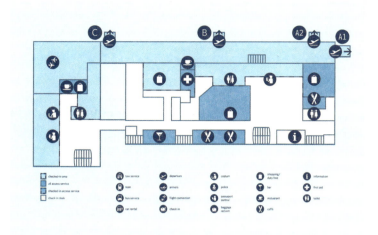

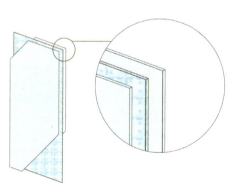

Partem para / **Departing to**
Johannesburg

RM 845

Status / **Status**
Na Hora / **On Time**

Embarque em / **Boarding at**
17:55 ●

Partem em / **Departing at**
18:30 ●

 Partidas Departures				**17.26** Monday, 13 June
Time	Destination	Flight	Gate	Remarks
18.30	Johannesburg	RM845	F10	**BOARDING**
18.30	Rome	FH786	F12	**BOARDING**
18.40	Madrid	MZ223	F24	**BOARDING**
18.45	Munchen	LU914	F17	Gate open
18.30	Johannesburg	RM845	F10	Gate open
18.30	Rome	FH786	F12	Gate open
18.40	Madrid	MZ223	F24	Gate open
18.45	Munchen	LU914	F17	Dlyd **19.20**
18.30	Johannesburg	RM845	F10	Dlyd **19.35**
18.30	Rome	FH786	F12	Dlyd **19.35**
18.40	Madrid	MZ223	F24	Dlyd **19.40**
18.45	Munchen	LU914	F17	
18.30	Johannesburg	RM845	F10	
18.30	Rome	FH786	F12	
18.40	Madrid	MZ223	F24	
18.45	Munchen	LU914	F17	
18.30	Johannesburg	RM845	F10	
18.30	Rome	FH786	F12	
18.40	Madrid	MZ223	F24	
18.45	Munchen	LU914	F17	
18.30	Johannesburg	RM845	F10	
18.30	Rome	FH786	F12	

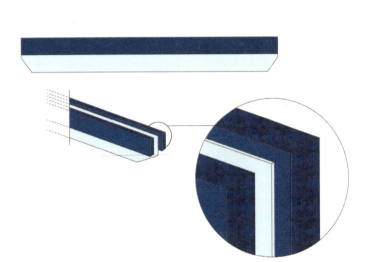

  Gates **Gates**   Gates **Gates**   Gates **Gates**

 Restaurante **Restaurant**   Shopping **Shopping**   Restaurante **Restaurant**

Partidas
Departures

Check-in
Check-in

Hotel Minho Signage System

Completion
2013

Design Agency
R2 Design

Designers
Lizá Defossez
Ramalho, Artur
Rebelo,
Artur Faria

Client
Hotel Minho

Location
Portugal

Photography
Eva Sousa,
Nélson Garrido

Located in Vila Nova de Cerveira, north of Portugal, Hotel Minho decided to renew its installations as well as the whole image. R2 was asked to create the new design concept, which should reflect the contemporaneity of the building and also the character of the region.

The designers were requested to create a signage system that should fit with the architecture project, and would interact and blend perfectly with the colour palette and materials. Their aim was to create a harmonious relationship between different materials, maintaining the aesthetic and consistent quality throughout the system.

The stag – symbol of the region was chosen as the identity's basilar sign and designed in various positions. The pictograms were designed based on the structure of the typeface Capibara (designed by Pieter van Rosmalen for Bold Monday, in 2008), and inspired by the letters of Theo van Doesburg. The elements were applied in the entire design project, which includes the corporate image as well as the signage system.

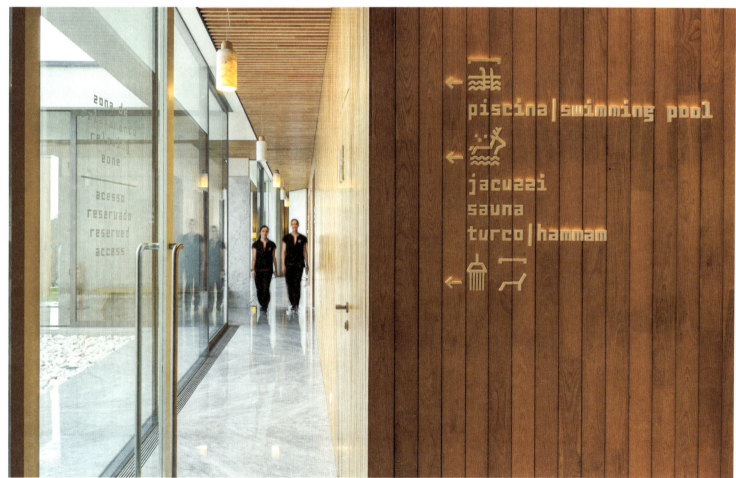

MGC Bistrica

Completion
2013
Design Agency
Studio 360
Designer
Vladan Srdic
Client
IMP d.d.
Location
Domžale, Slovenia
Photography
Studio 360

MGC Bistrica is a senior-citizen resort located in Domžale, Slovenia. Studio 360 was challenged to develop a complex visual identity consisting of different online / offline promotional materials and a signage system for the resort building. Since the primary target-group were old people, the designers developed a graphical language adjusted to their needs and emotions (pleasant, positive, colorful, cozy), easy recognition and interface usability.

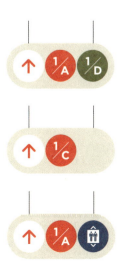

Ant Wayfinding System for Mt. Davis Youth Hostel

Completion
2012

Design Agency
Hong Kong Design Institute

Designers
HO Wing Yan, LEUNG Sze Wai

Client
Jockey ClubMt. Davis Youth Hostel

Location
Hong Kong, China

Photography
LEUNG Sze Wai

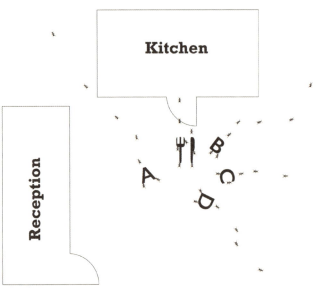

In the project, the Jockey Club Mt. Davis Youth Hostel hope they can give a good suggestion of wayfinding design. For concepts, they can see some ants climb in the youth hostel. Ants are a part of nature, also they are a part of hostel.

Actually, ants never get lost. For wayfinding, they are good images and directors for the customers who are confused. Ants are social insects. In a gregarious society of the ants, they need exchange and communication with each others as customers who are from different background exchange with each others in youth hostel.

有電
禁止內進

Banned from entering
Danger-Electricity

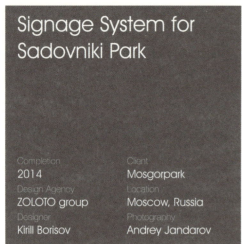

Signage System for Sadovniki Park

Completion	Client
2014	**Mosgorpark**
Design Agency	Location
ZOLOTO group	**Moscow, Russia**
Designer	Photography
Kirill Borisov	**Andrey Jandarov**

ZOLOTO group was tasked with developing a system to navigate Gardeners in such a way that it could be replicated and rescaled for other Moscow parks that are awaiting such an overhaul.

Over the course of the project, they designed a modular system, which became the basis of the constructive, graphic and informational content of the concept. The module elements have to be universal and convenient to use. The materials work well with the architectural elements of the park facilities, which are based on solid wood and stainless steel. Today the park has been completely renovated and the facilities are connected with a universal navigation system, used by thousands of visitors every day.

Gardens by the Bay

Completion
2012
Design Agency
Thomas.Matthews Communication Design
Designer
Thomas.Matthews Communication Design
Client
Grant Associates
Location
Singapore
Photography
Thomas.Matthews&Craig Sheppard

Gardens by the Bay is one of the largest garden projects of its kind in the world. Located on reclaimed land in Singapore's new downtown at Marina Bay, the site provides a unique leisure destination for local and international visitors.

The Garden's identity pattern took its lead from the stars of the garden; the flora and fauna. The studio worked closely with the master planning team to help create an identity that worked not only on the communication media but also, within architecture, landscape, packaging and even the tour bus.

Regular icons

Regular icons (reversed)

Square icons

Square icons (reversed)

Cautionary icons

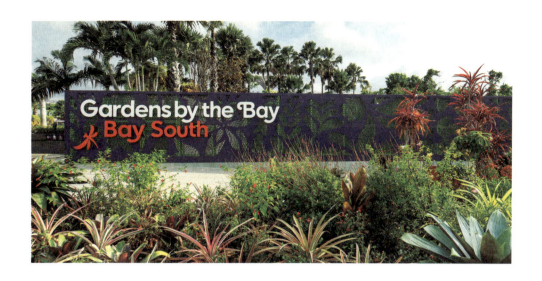

The Meadows
Padang Rumput
冷乾 溫室冷

Amazing Fruits and Flowers Amazing Buah-buahan Dan 獅子林子 林獅子林		↙
Supertrees Super Pohon 獅子林子 林獅子林	🛗 🍴🌳	↘
Dragonfly Lake Capung Tasik 獅子林子 林獅子林		↘
Toilets Toilets 獅子林子	🚹🚺♿👶	←
Restaurant Restoran 獅子林子	🍴	←
Lily Pond Lily Kolam 獅子林子	✚	↖
Kingfisher Lake Tasik Kingfisher 獅子林子		↖
Arrival Square Kedatangan Persegi 獅子林子		↗

Amazing Fruits and Flowers
Amazing Buah-buahan Dan
冷乾 溫室冷

Exit Keluar 獅子林		↘
Supertrees Super Pohon 獅子林獅子	🛗🍴🌳	↘
Reception Perimaan 獅子林獅子	ℹ	↘
Toilets Toilets 獅子林	🚹🚺♿👶	↘
Restaurant Restaurant 獅子林子	🍴	←
Lily Pond Lily Kolam 獅子林子		↗
Kingfisher Lake Tasik Kingfisher 獅子林子		↗

Amazing Fruits and Flowers
Amazing Buah-buahan Dan
冷乾 溫室冷

Toilets Toilets 獅子林	🚹🚺♿👶	←
Restaurant Restaurant 獅子林子	🍴	←
Lily Pond Lily Kolam 獅子林子	✚	↗
Kingfisher Lake Tasik Kingfisher 獅子林子		↗

Restaurant Restaurant 獅子林子	🚹🚺♿👶🍴	←
Lily Pond Lily Kolam 獅子林子	✚	↗
Kingfisher Lake Tasik Kingfisher 獅子林子		↗

The Meadows
Padang Rumput
冷乾 溫室冷

Amazing Fruits and Flowers Amazing Buah-buahan Dan 獅子林子 林獅子林		↙
Supertrees Super Pohon 獅子林子 林獅子林	🛗🍴🌳	↘
Dragonfly Lake Capung Tasik 獅子林子 林獅子林		↘
Toilets Toilets 獅子林子	🚹🚺♿👶	←
Restaurant Restoran 獅子林子	🍴	←
Lily Pond Lily Kolam 獅子林子	✚	↖
Kingfisher Lake Tasik Kingfisher 獅子林子		↖
Arrival Square Kedatangan Persegi 獅子林子		↗

The Meadows
Padang Rumput
冷乾 溫室冷

Amazing Fruits and Flowers Amazing Buah-buahan Dan 獅子林子 林獅子林		↙
Supertrees Super Pohon 獅子林子 林獅子林	🛗🍴🌳	↘
Dragonfly Lake Capung Tasik 獅子林子 林獅子林		↘
Toilets Toilets 獅子林子	🚹🚺♿👶	←
Restaurant Restoran 獅子林子	🍴	←
Lily Pond Lily Kolam 獅子林子	✚	↖
Kingfisher Lake Tasik Kingfisher 獅子林子		↖
Arrival Square Kedatangan Persegi 獅子林子		↗

In response to the challenge of representing the massively diverse environment, and taking inspiration from the multi-layered Singaporean culture, the eastern craft of paper-cutting and the paintings of Rousseau (the client's favourite artist), the designers developed an intricate and organic 'brand pattern'. The pattern cleverly conceals wildlife that can be found in the gardens, and the process of discovering them suitably reflects the wonder of the natural world that the project evokes.

This diverse pattern has been cropped, abstracted, tessellated and implemented through all communication channels and used extensively through the garden wayfinding, and on merchandising. It has been laser cut into back-lit signage, used as filigree patterns in shelters as well as textile designs for scarves and tote bags. The studio developed two cuts of typeface with complimentary icon designs.

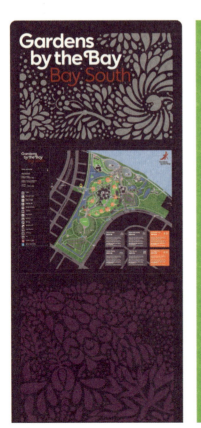

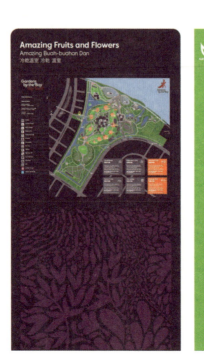

Wayfinding Project for Reserva el Peñón

Completion
2015
Designer
Jani Rivera
Client
Reserva el Peñón
Location
Valle de Bravo
Photography
Alejandro Filloy

Reserva el Peñón is a real state project in Valle de Bravo, México. This project has been successfully combining environmental, social and economic approaches to create and enhance a spatial experience of site and infrastructure.

SEÑALIZACIÓN DE CAMINOS

- Viga de madera del sitio de 120 cm de altura y de 20 x 21 cm.
- Plano de 20 x 21 cm.
- Presentado a 20°.
- Plano general calado, electropintado y serigrafiado.
- Nombre del camino y/o sendero calado y electropintado.

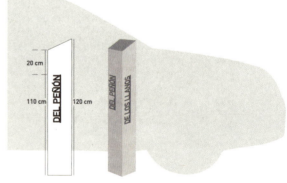

SEÑALIZACIÓN DE SENDEROS

- Viga de 62.5 cm de altura con corte a 20°.
- Nombre del sendero pintado con esténcil.

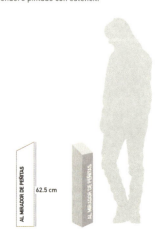

This development has two kinds of roads: main roads for cars, and trails for walking. The designers worked together to create this signage family on two levels:

1. Long distance signage perceptible from within the car offering large-scale and wide-area orientation.

2. Pedestrian signage on a smaller scale which guides walkers to all the common areas through smaller and natural trails. The designers tried to use the wood of sick trees in the site to elaborate the structure of the signage and to incorporate them to the natural landscape. The colour palette was chosen considering the colours of the vegetation.

Wayfinding: 100 NYC Public Sculptures

Completion
2014
Designer
Bundith Phunsombatlert
Location
New York, USA

 6.77 mi

 6.66 mi

 17.39 mi

 0.04 mi

 8.45 mi

 7.36 mi

 7.12 mi

 1.47 mi

 7.36 mi

 9.92 mi

 5.29 mi

 8.05 mi

This interdisciplinary work combines the practice of printmaking in old media with one of technology in a new media: the use of GPS coordinates, a digital compass, and an online map. This solution transforms the definition of public art by introducing a more robust component of exploration and navigation. In addition, the work will activate new definitions of original mapped sculptures. Their established meanings will be changed as they are discussed by people face-to-face at the sites or online through social networks, bringing them to life in new media. Wayfinding: 100 NYC Public Sculptures engages the public to interpret the original work through their physical journeys, experiences, and memories.

Brooklyn Botanic Gardens

Completion
2015

Design Agency
C&G Partners

Designers
Keith Helmetag,
Partner-in-Charge
Amy Siegel,
Partner & Lead Sign
Designer

Client
Brooklyn Botanic
Gardens

Location
USA

Photography
au2026

Japanese Hill-and-Pond Garden

When it opened in 1915, this was the first Japanese-inspired garden within an American public garden. Considered a masterpiece of landscape designer Takeo Shiota, it offers harmonious views from every angle and beauty in all seasons.

The balance of natural and man-made beauty is the basis of this garden. A blend of two Japanese styles, the ancient "hill-and-pond" garden and modern "stroll" garden, elements like the rocks and waterfall have been carefully positioned, and trees here reveal decades of artful pruning.

Stroll the garden.
The winding path reveals a new perspective at every turn.

Find cultural elements.
The red structure in the pond is a Torii, which indicates the presence of the shrine on the hill beyond. The shrine is dedicated to the Shinto deity Inari, protector of plants.

Please
Do not feed the animals or throw anything into the pond. Keep to the path but don't block it. Make sure children stay with an adult caregiver.

Over the years the garden has evolved however key elements, such as the torii gate seen here in 1916, have been here since the beginning.

C&G Partners has recently collaborated with the Brooklyn Botanic Garden on a comprehensive orientation, directional wayfinding and mapping system. Occurring over multiple phases, the rollout updates an ad-hoc assortment of placemaking signs, directional signs and other elements that have developed over the Garden's extensive history without a central design directive.

The new signs feature sleek, polished porcelain enamel faces, and set within weathered bronze armatures that evoke the Garden's austere, late 19th century fixtures, with stark directional lettering providing an instantly recognisable graphic contrast to the lushness of the grounds.

The central feature of the program is the Garden's new maps. With stylistically evocative of the lush watercolors that are a Garden tradition, the new map is a fully digital production, able to incorporate future changes in the landscape or nomenclature with a minimum of change. Whether seen physically on the grounds, encountered as a digital installation in the Visitor Centre, or used in a future app, the Garden Maps will grow and expand along with the Garden for many years to come.

Rock Garden

Created in 1917 and expanded in 1992, this boulder-strewn slope showcases compact plants suited for growing in shallow, arid soils.

Other than those growing around the pond, all the plants here need good drainage and little water. The microclimates created by the placement of glacial boulders within this garden provide special conditions for a wide variety of species. See what's growing in the sunny, dry beds; shady woodland areas; and the ericaceous bed, which has acidic soil.

This garden displays some of the earliest signs of spring as well as brilliant color in the fall.

Woodland

Acid-Loving Plants

Conifers

Shade-Tolerant Plants

▼ To Herb Garden

To ▼ Oak Circle

📍 **Get ideas.**
The Rock Garden features a variety of tough plants that grow well in small spaces, such as the native Eastern prickly-pear cactus, which produces pretty flowers and edible fruit.

🔍 **Notice adaptations.**
Plant species living in low-water conditions have evolved interesting ways to get the moisture they need. A few adaptations to look for: waxy, small, or hairy leaves.

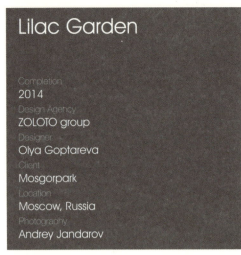

Lilac Garden

Completion
2014
Design Agency
ZOLOTO group
Designer
Olya Goptareva
Client
Mosgorpark
Location
Moscow, Russia
Photography
Andrey Jandarov

Lilac Garden is a museum of lilacs under an open sky. The navigation system in this park is designed to provide visitors with information about the different varieties of lilacs. They placed a system of stands in the park that contain interesting passages about the types of plants.

With the help of numbering system and colour-coding, visitors can easily find the lilacs which attract the most interest of them. The stands and signs are made of metal that is painted lilac, carved with signature patterns – the low openwork design fits well into the landscape and keeps these from looking bulky. In developing the navigation system for the park, they deliberately abandoned strict graphical icons and a dry formulation of rules for behavior, and instead placed plaques around the garden with information and friendly reminders for visitors.

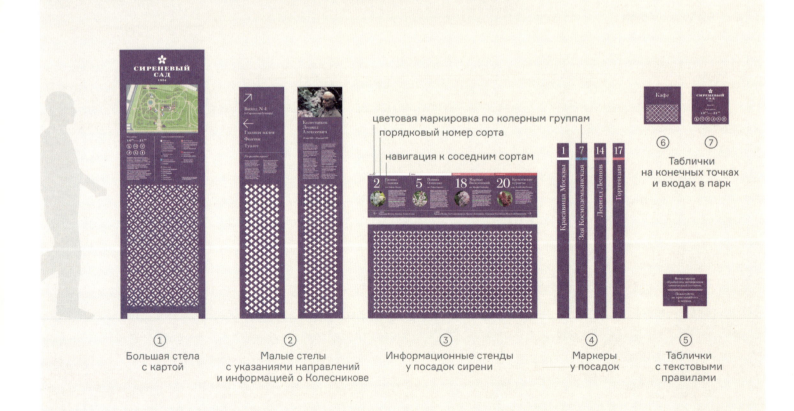

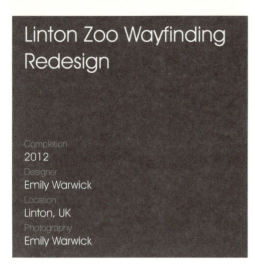

Linton Zoo Wayfinding Redesign

Completion
2012
Designer
Emily Warwick
Location
Linton, UK
Photography
Emily Warwick

The designer redesigned the wayfinding system used at Linton Zoological Gardens. The current design and layout of the zoo's wayfinding system have no consistent style or design, so the designer focused on making a consistent design, which helps highlight each area of the zoo for easier use and better understanding.

WARNING
Do not feed
the animals

WARNING
Open
water

WARNING
Do not feed
the animals

ATTENTION
Children must be
supervised at all
times

Cafe

Cafe

Picnic & Play Area

Undercover Area

Gift Shop

Toilets

African Lion

Hornbill

Giant Tortoises

Dinsoaurs

Lemurs

Parrots

African Lion

Brazilian Tapir

Thiago and Tiana

(Also known as : Lowland Tapir, South American Tapir, Anta)

We live here

La Molina Signage

Completion
2013
Designers
Adrià Gómez, Sergi Diaz, Jaume Juan
Client
EASD Serra i Abella
Location
Barcelona, Spain
Photography
Jaume Juan

This is a wayfinding system for the mountain trail 732 in La Molina, Catalonia. The colour used for the signs is black, a pretty unusual one in signage. The choice of colour is for the integration on the environment, giving prominence to the vivid colour pictograms.

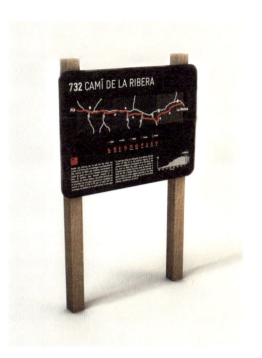

 DESNIVELL
 PATRIMONI
 TORRENT
 LA MOLINA

 INFORMACIÓ
 KM 5
 ESTRENYIMENT
 ALP

 PI ROIG
 AVET BLANC
 AVET COMÚ
 MORFOLOGIA

Dartington Estate
Signage & Wayfinding

Completion
2013
Design Agency
Sames+Littlejohns
Client
Dartington Hall Trust
Location
Devon, UK
Photography
David Sames

Dartington Estate is a 1,200 acre site that is home to a listed medieval hall, courtyard and 25 acres of Grade 2 listed Gardens. Open all year round to the public, development of a complete signage and wayfinding scheme was commissioned to help improve and enhance the overall visitor experience. The scope of works involved in the Delivery of the Scheme; Research & Analysis; Strategy & Planning, Design, Production and Installation.

Frome Street Bikeway Signage

Completion	Client
2014	City of Adelaide
Designers	**Location**
Ian Rooney,	Adelaide, Australia
Angela Arango,	**Photography**
Laura Cornhill	Don Brice
Design Agency	
ASPECT studios	

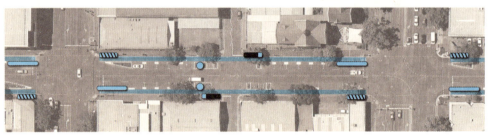

A to B Wayfinding was engaged to carry out a wayfinding strategy for a new bikeway in Frome Street, Adelaide. The bikeway is an opportunity to promote cycling as a viable mode of transport to the city and therefore required a legible and visually engaging visual language to promote the route. Building on the City wide Wayfinding Strategy, the cycle signage included branding elements, mid block and intersection directional information on island separators and sign panels collocated to existing light poles. Consistent placement of information for cyclists meant delivering the right information at the right time whilst providing a safe and comfortable experience for bikeway users. A cost effective approach to wayfinding was implemented using affordable materials and production methods including poles wrapped in stickers and surface decals.

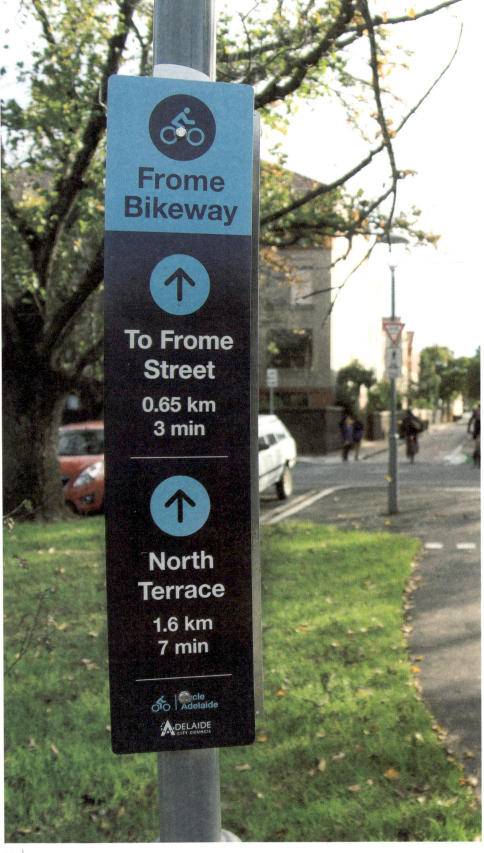

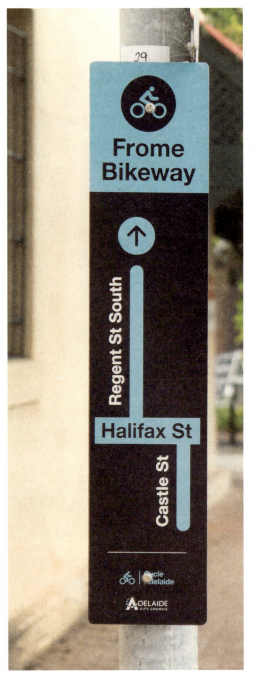

Guerilla – Occupy the Tourist Guidance of Berlin

Completion
2014
Designers
Christian Pannicke, Paul Eschenbach
Location
Berlin, Germany
Photography
Christian Pannicke

Guerilla is a student project of the University of Applied Sciences Berlin, Department of Communication Design, under the direction of Prof. Florian Adler. Every team got a way of 1 kilometer in the area of Berlin. They had to check out every way they could walk from the starting point to target, to count all signages on the way and to analyse what was missing to inform and orientate. Every team had to find out the best solution.

← Haus der Berliner Festspiele	800m
← Zoo / Gedächtniskirche	700m
← Käthe-Kollwitz-Museum	300m

Kurfürstendamm

Maison de France	5 min
Jüdisches Gemeindehaus	5 min
Haus der Berliner Festspiele	7 min

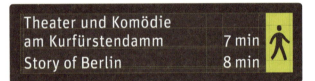

| Theater und Komödie am Kurfürstendamm | 7 min |
| Story of Berlin | 8 min |

| Story of Berlin | 7 min |
| Theater und Komödie am Kurfürstendamm | 8 min |

© Senatsverwaltung für Stadtentwicklung und Umwelt, Berlin und Grün Berlin GmbH

← Zoo / Aquarium	800m
← Europa Center	450m
← Kaiser-Wilhelm-Gedächtniskirche	300m

← Museum für Fotografie	550m
← Helmut Newton Museum	550m
← Zoo Haupteingang	550m

| → Story of Berlin | 650m |
| → Theater und Komödie am Kurfürstendamm | 450m |

← Erotikmuseum	200m
← 🛈	100m
← Haus der Berliner Festspiele	650m

→ Museum für Fotografie	550m
→ Helmut Newton Museum	550m
Zoo Haupteingang	550m

Kaiser-Wilhelm-Gedächtniskirche	4 min
Zoo Haupteingang	7 min
Europacenter	8 min

Maison de France	5 min
Jüdisches Gemeindehaus	5 min
Haus der Berliner Festspiele	7 min

Erotikmuseum	4 min
Museum für Fotografie	8 min
Helmut Newton Museum	8 min

| Theater und Komödie am Kurfürstendamm | 7 min |
| Story of Berlin | 8 min |

The designers got the Kurfüstendamm in Charlottenburg. At the beginning it required an analysis of the existing communication media in public space of Berlin. The result was a quantitative as well as qualitative oversupply of visual stimuli without consistent guidance. Based on the studies, a concept was developed for the signage of the city through an exemplary path. Existing carriers were occupied: The tourist signposting of Berlin was completely redesigned graphically by expanding orientation and information system, which was installed on the billboards of the company wall.

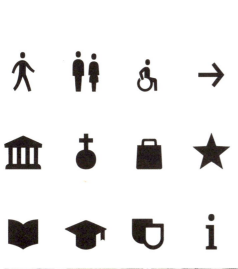

Qantas Mascot Campus

Completion
2014

Client
Qantas Airways

Design Agency
Frost*collective

Location
NSW, Australia

Designer
Carlo Giannasca

Photography
Ant Geernaert

The signage developed by Frost*, which includes large-scale, illuminated letterforms to identify the buildings within the campus, is intended to be simple, elegant and premium. Based on an abstraction of the idea of a 'journey', the forms are soft, organic and contemporary, with curved edges. An elegant and restrained materials palette, including frosted acrylic Perspex and satin-finished, anodized aluminium, is utilised throughout the campus.

The basic construction of the signs includes an aluminium frame that encases a frosted acrylic sheet which inturn is illuminated by a matrix of LEDs that sit below the surface. The result is signage that literally shines like a beacon, guiding users around the building. The graphics are applied vinyl die-cut lettering rendered in two shades of grey, designed to facilitate changeability.

Hudson Fysh Street

→ A Wing
Meeting Suite

↑ B Wing
IT Kiosk
Training Suite
Wellness Centre
Paul McGinness Cabin

↑ Fergus McMaster
Backyard

← C Wing
James Strong
Auditorium

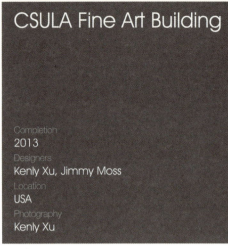

CSULA Fine Art Building

Completion
2013
Designers
Kenly Xu, Jimmy Moss
Location
USA
Photography
Kenly Xu

The wayfinding project is designed for the old Fine Art building in CSULA. This structural shape often confuses new students and guests. And, the numbering system even makes the confusion complex. This conceptual wayfinding system is designed based on the reversed colour palette of CSULA and shapes of warning sign on streets. By placing the signs on both sides in the hallway, people can easily filter out and locate the room they are looking for. With directory placed at each decision point, people wouldn't need to walk back and forth like before.

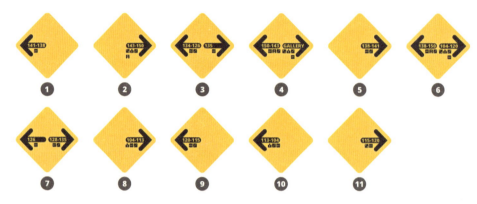

LEVEL 1

Gallery	
Sculpture Studio	
Ceramic Studio	106 & 107
Painting Studio	108
COMA Gallery	115
Technical Support	126A
Health & Human Service Dean	126
CETL Lab	130
	138

LEVEL 2

Drawing Studio	206
LACHSA Visual Arts	215
Spray Booth Room	222
Printmaking Studio	223
Animation Studio	225
Computer Graphic Studio	226
Health & Human Service Advisement Center	238
Fashion & Textile Studio	239

LEVEL 3

Blueprint Lab	307
Mixed Media Studio	316
Design Woodshop	317
Undergraduate Studio	320
Art Dept. Student Service	326
Art Dept. Adminstration	328
Mailroom	330
Art Dept. Visual Resource	332
Art Seminar Room	333

2

LEVEL 1

Gallery	
Sculpture Studio	106 & 107
Ceramic Studio	108
Painting Studio	115
COMA Gallery	126A
Technical Support	126
Health & Human Service Dean	130
CETL Lab	138

LEVEL 2

Drawing Studio	206
LACHSA Visual Arts	215
Spray Booth Room	222
Printmaking Studio	223
Animation Studio	225
Computer Graphic Studio	226
Health & Human Service Advisement Center	238
Fashion & Textile Studio	239

LEVEL 3

Blueprint Lab	307
Mixed Media Studio	316
Design Woodshop	317
Undergraduate Studio	320
Art Dept. Student Service	326
Art Dept. Adminstration	328
Mailroom	330
Art Dept. Visual Resource	332
Art Seminar Room	333

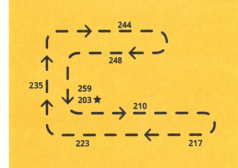

1 2 3

LEVEL 1

Gallery	
Sculpture Studio	106 & 107
Ceramic Studio	108
Painting Studio	115
COMA Gallery	126A
Technical Support	126
Health & Human Service Dean	130
CETL Lab	138

LEVEL 2

Drawing Studio	206
LACHSA Visual Arts	215
Spray Booth Room	222
Printmaking Studio	223
Animation Studio	225
Computer Graphic Studio	226
Health & Human Service Advisement Center	238
Fashion & Textile Studio	239

LEVEL 3

Blueprint Lab	307
Mixed Media Studio	316
Design Woodshop	317
Undergraduate Studio	320
Art Dept. Student Service	326
Art Dept. Adminstration	328
Mailroom	330
Art Dept. Visual Resource	332
Art Seminar Room	333

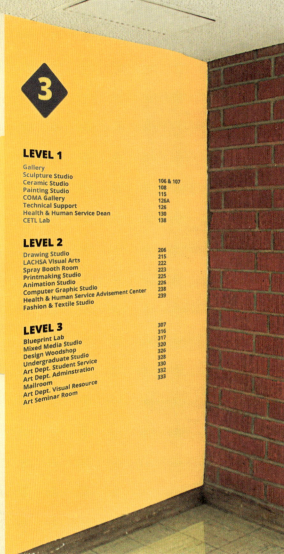

3

LEVEL 1

Gallery	
Sculpture Studio	
Ceramic Studio	106 & 107
Painting Studio	108
COMA Gallery	115
Technical Support	126A
Health & Human Service Dean	126
CETL Lab	130
	138

LEVEL 2

Drawing Studio	206
LACHSA Visual Arts	215
Spray Booth Room	222
Printmaking Studio	223
Animation Studio	225
Computer Graphic Studio	226
Health & Human Service Advisement Center	238
Fashion & Textile Studio	239

LEVEL 3

Blueprint Lab	307
Mixed Media Studio	316
Design Woodshop	317
Undergraduate Studio	320
Art Dept. Student Service	326
Art Dept. Adminstration	328
Mailroom	330
Art Dept. Visual Resource	332
Art Seminar Room	333

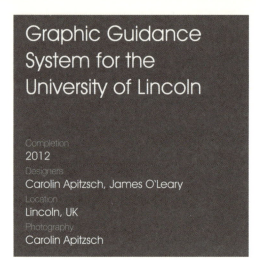

Graphic Guidance System for the University of Lincoln

Completion
2012
Designers
Carolin Apitzsch, James O'Leary
Location
Lincoln, UK
Photography
Carolin Apitzsch

Carolin Apitzsch generated a guidance system for the School of Art, Architecture and Design building of the University of Lincoln. The building was designed by RICK MATHER ARCHITECTS and reflects absolute simplicity by a creamy white sculptural form. More than 400 people pass the building every day, most of which are students.

The designer decided to split the guidance system in three sections. A digital screen near the entry presents important information for students like a personal timetable, canteen offers, meetings or room occupation. The second part provides digital maps, which are intended for visitors. Whenever someone passes a designated area, a motion detector triggers the projection of a map on the wall. Last but not least the designer planned a clear and coherent naming of each room.

G KITCHEN CAFETERIA

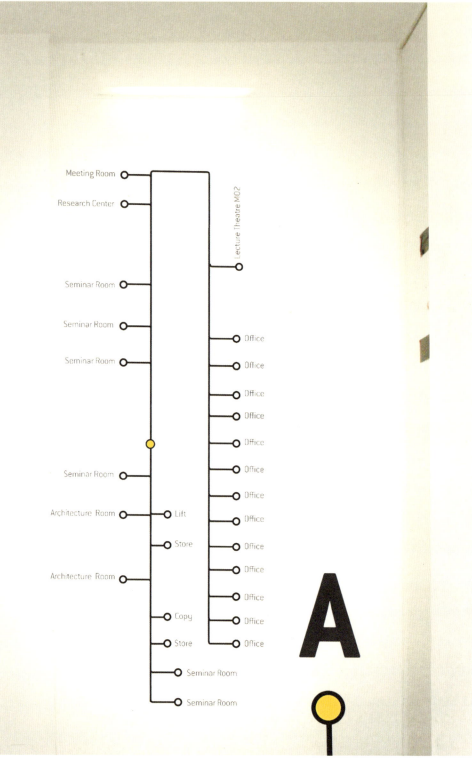

Ⓐ Studio 001: A Floor, Architecture Studio
1. Level course, BA (Hons) Architecture

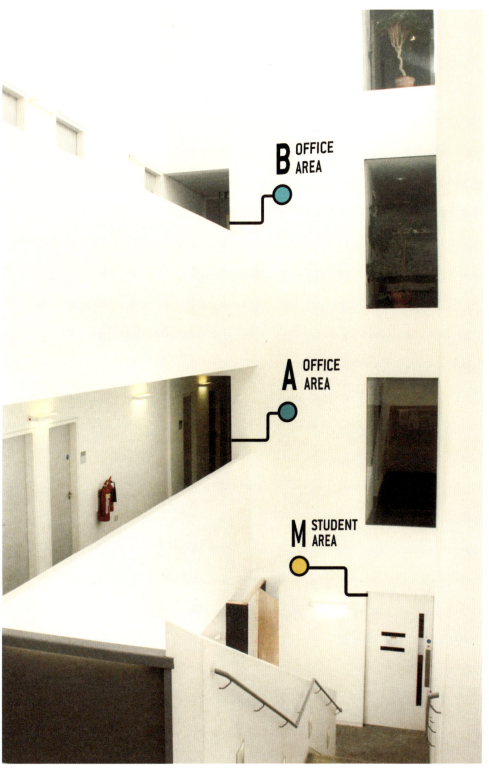

B OFFICE AREA

A OFFICE AREA

A OFFICE AREA

M STUDENT AREA

R.I.B.A   Studio, Lecture Theatre, Seminar Room   Workshop, Print   Office, Meeting Room

PLEASE TOUCH ME

Wayfinding System 1 for London College of Contemporary Arts

Completion
2014
Designer
Pelin Morris
Client
London College of Contemporary Arts
Location
London, UK
Photography
Pelin Morris

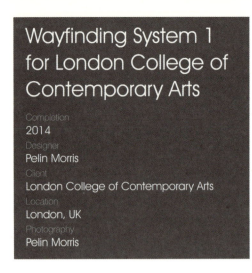

This wayfinding system was implemented to create a strong contemporary identity for London College of Contemporary Arts' Holborn campus.

The system is communicating the same contemporary graphic language as the identity of the art college. Design concept was inspired by the college's convex shaped Logo. All the floors are "shape-coded", each floor has its own convex shape.

Following the successful implementation of the brand identity across the wayfinding system, the visual identity continues on the walls within the college. The signage system allows visitors to navigate better in the college and acts as the visual glue that holds the building together.

Wayfinding System 2 for London College of Contemporary Arts

Completion
2013
Designer
Pelin Morris
Client
London College of Contemporary Arts
Location
London, UK
Photography
Pelin Morris

This project is developed for an Art College in Soho, London, which specialises in design and fashion. The main aim was to create an effective and clear wayfinding system which also makes a bold statement.

The floor numbers, wrapped at the corner on the walls, provide a modern environment that is both inspirational and striking. The floors are identified with big bold colourful numbers and are functional in terms of being easily recognisable and readable from different directions. The design helped to define spaces clearly and added a unique personality to the art college.

4 Fashion Studio 1
Senior Academic
MD & Executive
👫

3 Lecture Room 3
Mac Studio 2 &
Lectra Room
👫

2 Cinema Studio
Canteen & Loun
Mac Studio 1
Lecture Room 2
👫

1 Lecture Room 1
Foundation Stud
Administration O
QAA / Academic
👫

3 Lecture Room 3
Mac Studio 2 & 3
Lectra Room
👫

2 Cinema Studio
Canteen & Lounge Area
Mac Studio 1
Lecture Room 2
👫

1 Lecture Room 1
Foundation Studio
Administration Office
QAA / Academic Office
👫

G Gallery
Art Shop
Reception
Photo Studio 1, 2 & 3
Photography Faculty Office
👫

Dark Room

4 Fashion Studio 1 & 2
Senior Academic Office
MD & Executive Dean's O

3 Lecture Room 3
Mac Studio 2 & 3
Lectra Room

2 Cinema S
Canteen &
Mac Studi
Lecture Ro

5 Fashion Studio 3
Fashion Faculty Office

4 Fashion Studio 1 & 2
Senior Academic Office
MD & Executive Dean's Office

3 Lecture Room 3
Mac Studio 2 & 3
Lectra Room

2 Cinema Studio
Canteen & Lounge Area
Mac Studio 1
Lecture Room 2

1 Lecture Room 1
Foundation Studio
Administration Office
QAA / Academic Office

G Gallery
Art Shop
Reception
Photo Studio 1, 2 & 3
Photography Faculty Office

B Photography Dark Room
Photography Suite
Boardroom
Recruitment and Admissions
Library and Study Area
Finance Office

5 Fashion Studio 3
Fashion Faculty Office

Technical University Berlin

Completion
2014

Design Agency
Plural

Designers
Kilian Krug, Ivy Kunze, Sharmila Sandrasegar

Client
Technische Universität Berlin

Location
Berlin, Germany

Photography
Kilian Krug

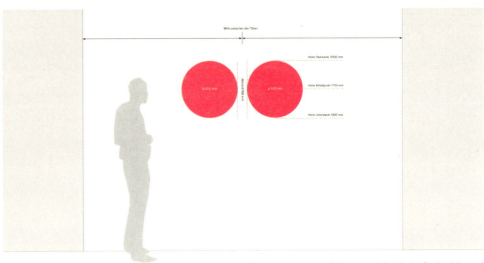

The architecture of the new Marchstraße building of the Technical University (Berlin's largest university) use modern, industrial architecture of the early 20th century for reference. To emphasise this characteristic of the architecture, Plural designed an orientation system resembling the tin-plate signs of factory buildings and coloured pink to reflect the vibrant student life. The resulting bright dots that comprise the signs are highly visible for leading the visitors through the building.

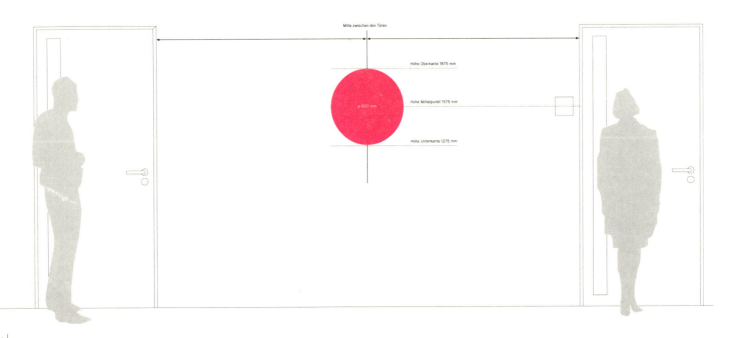

Completion
2013
Designer
Hannah Headrick
Client
Queensland College of Art assignment
Location
Brisbane, Australia
Photography
Hannah Headrick

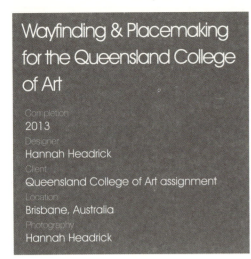

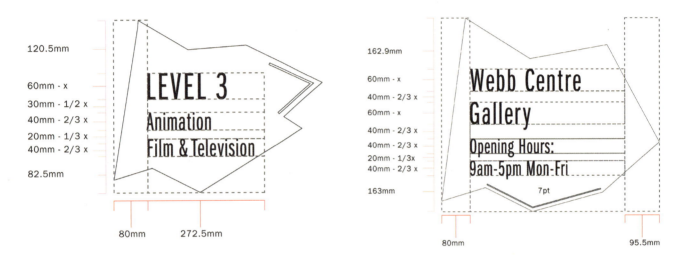

120.5mm

60mm - x
30mm - 1/2 x
40mm - 2/3 x
20mm - 1/3 x
40mm - 2/3 x

82.5mm

LEVEL 3
Animation
Film & Television

80mm   272.5mm

162.9mm

60mm - x
40mm - 2/3 x
60mm - x
40mm - 2/3 x
40mm - 2/3 x
20mm - 1/3x
40mm - 2/3 x

163mm

Webb Centre
Gallery
Opening Hours:
9am-5pm Mon-Fri

7pt

80mm   95.5mm

QCA, the Queensland College of Art, is a university campus full of creative students from various disciplines, with many notable alumni as well. However, the location of the campus and the works of the students are both relatively unknown. Through applying an appropriate wayfinding system and creating a sense of place, QCA should become not only a university that the students are attached to, but a university that frequently encourages members of the public to visit, hopefully turning the campus into a local art icon. It is hoped that this will be achieved through transforming the campus into an art hub through large-scale artworks adorning the walls, better areas to display student work, and a modern art gallery aesthetic-themed wayfinding system. Another element that could make QCA an icon is the existence of a green roof-an environmentally-friendly, animal attracting feature. This would also strengthen QCA's ties to sustainability.

LEVEL 5
Board Room
Provost & Director

LEVEL 4
Art Theory
Fine Art
Research Office

LEVEL 3
Animation
Film and Television

LEVEL 2
Design

LEVEL 1
Learning Centre

LEVEL 0
Campus Life
Project Gallery
Gumumil Centre

LEVEL -1
Parking

S05
Lecture Theatre
& Gallery

LEVEL 2
Design

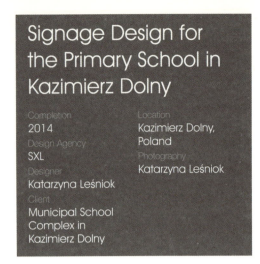

Signage Design for the Primary School in Kazimierz Dolny

Completion
2014
Design Agency
SXL
Designer
Katarzyna Leśniok
Client
Municipal School
Complex in
Kazimierz Dolny

Location
Kazimierz Dolny,
Poland
Photography
Katarzyna Leśniok

The visual information system consists of three types of applications: basic information (designation for every room in the school), directional information (a set of pictograms with arrows showing the direction of a desirable destination) and complementary information (depending on the purpose of the room, it is either a pictogram or the name of the classroom beginning with the first letter in a large size).

The height of the basic information applications is equal of the height of an adult's eyes. Complementary information is on the height that is appropriate for children (60 centimetres) and it is in a bigger scale so that it can be more visible. Directional information is easily accessible to both types of users. A special set of pictograms referring to a chosen typeface was prepared as a part of the project.

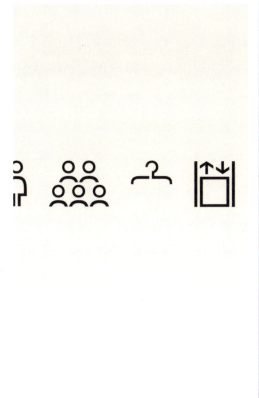

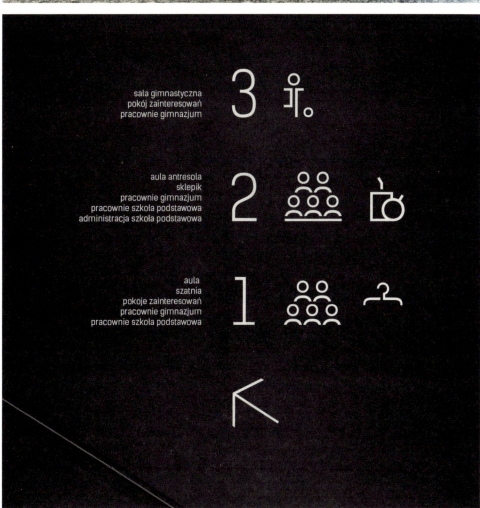

sala gimnastyczna
pokój zainteresowań
pracownie gimnazjum

3

aula antresola
sklepik
pracownie gimnazjum
pracownie szkoła podstawowa
administracja szkoła podstawowa

2

aula
szatnia
pokoje zainteresowań
pracownie gimnazjum
pracownie szkoła podstawowa

1

Indus Valley School of Art and Architecture (IVS) Thesis Display

Completion
2014
Designer
Sakina Shoaib Ali
Client
IVS
Location
Karachi, Pakistan
Photography
Sakina Shoaib Ali

A fun / colourful wayfinding system for an art schools thesis displays showcasing four departments. The objective was to create something simple and sustainable that could be used as a permanent system eventually. This system used color codes and lines which one simply has to follow to reach their specific department / destination.

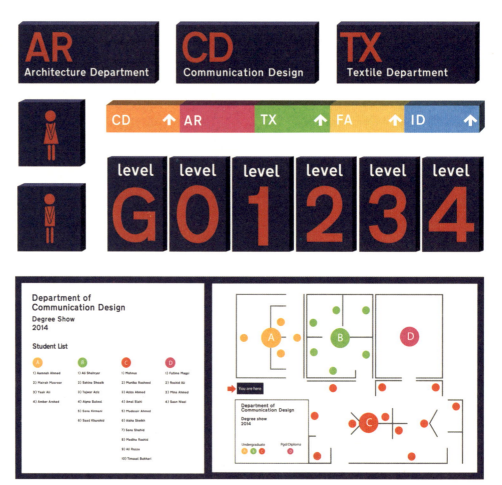

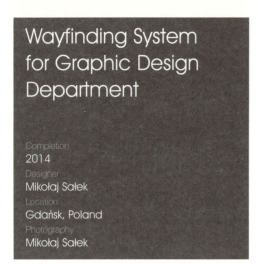

Wayfinding System for Graphic Design Department

Completion
2014
Designer
Mikołaj Sałek
Location
Gdańsk, Poland
Photography
Mikołaj Sałek

The main idea of this project was to create a visual map and wayfinding for graphic design workshops. He started from creating modular diagonal grid based on the arrow-direction of movement. Rest of the elements like a map or pictograms were designed on this grid. Project in its assumption is simple and contrastive.

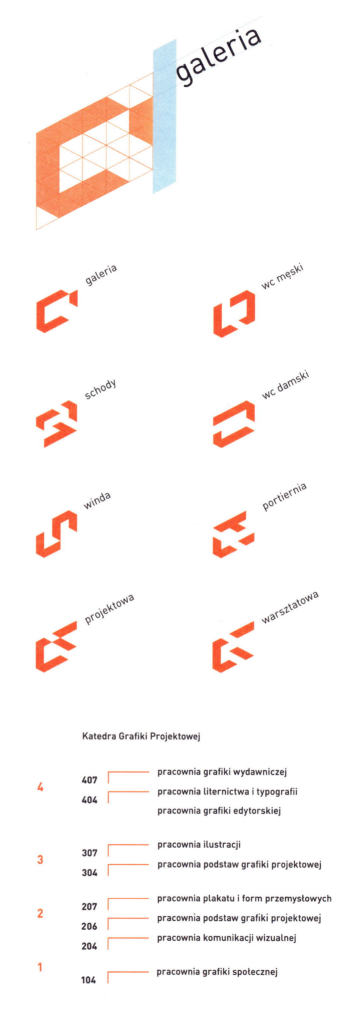

galeria

galeria

wc męski

schody

wc damski

winda

portiernia

projektowa

warsztatowa

Katedra Grafiki Projektowej

4	407	pracownia grafiki wydawniczej
	404	pracownia liternictwa i typografii
		pracownia grafiki edytorskiej
3	307	pracownia ilustracji
	304	pracownia podstaw grafiki projektowej
2	207	pracownia plakatu i form przemysłowych
	206	pracownia podstaw grafiki projektowej
	204	pracownia komunikacji wizualnej
1	104	pracownia grafiki społecznej

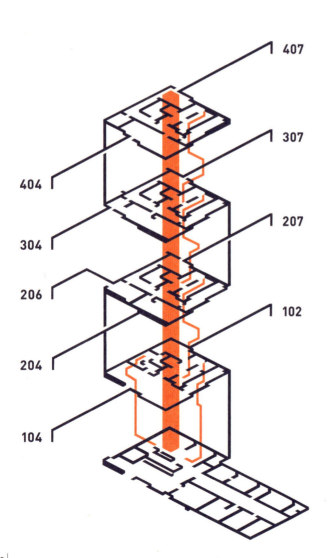

407
307
404
207
304
206
102
204
104

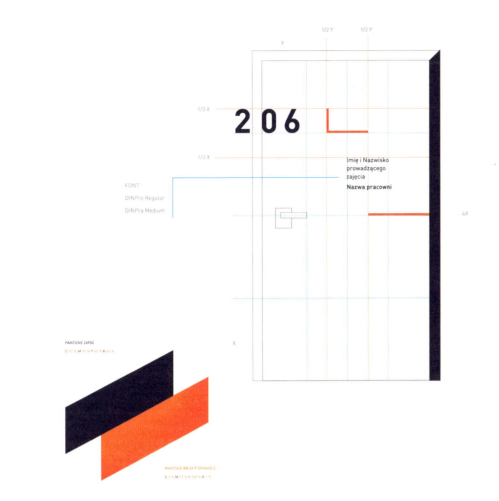

1/2 Y   1/2 Y

Y

1/3 X

2 0 6

1/3 X

FONT
DINPro Regular
DINPro Medium

Imię i Nazwisko
prowadzącego
zajęcia
Nazwa pracowni

4X

X

PANTONE 2695C
C 87 % M 95 % Y 40 % K 44 %

DINPro

Light
Regular
Medium
Bold
abcdefghijklm
noprstuqwxyz
0123456789

PANTONE BRIGHT ORANGE C
C 0 % M 77 % Y 100 % K 0 %

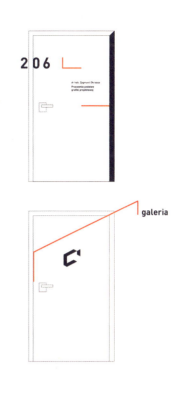

2 0 6

galeria

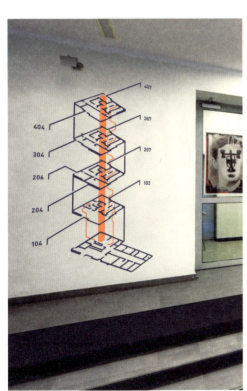

407
404
307
304
207
206
204
102
104

Katedra Grafiki Projektowej

4   407   pracownia grafiki wydawniczej
    404   pracownia liternictwa i typografii
          pracownia grafiki edytorskiej

3   307   pracownia ilustracji
    304   pracownia podstaw grafiki projektowej

2   207   pracownia plakatu i form przemysłowych
    206   pracownia podstaw grafiki projektowej
    204   pracownia komunikacji wizualnej

1   104   pracownia grafiki społecznej

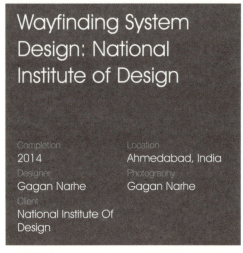

Wayfinding System Design: National Institute of Design

Completion	Location
2014	Ahmedabad, India
Designer	Photography
Gagan Narhe	Gagan Narhe
Client	
National Institute Of Design	

NATIONAL INSTITUTE of DESIGN, acclaimed one of the finest design institute and established in 1961, is an autonomous governing body which provides research service and training in Industrial design & visual communication.

The main campus situated in Ahmedabad, was known as heritage campus. The navigation system currently inside the campus is dated and not appropriate as it's the prime design institute in India. The current system has to reexamine, in order to make it up-to-date. The lack of modularity can be improved by using effective visual language, making the communication simpler, as there is a scope for betterment. The whole communication can be done in more interesting, informative & inclusive way.

ACTIVITY CENTER — # ed1c24
ACADEMICS — # f57e20
ADMINISTRATION — # 4e2b1e
RESOURCES — # 1d9b48
CONSULTANCY — # 3d51a3
UTILITIES — # 762f92
COMMON — #15b4a1

Color Coding

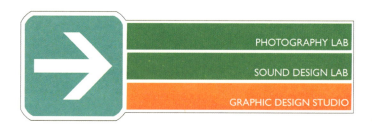

PHOTOGRAPHY LAB
SOUND DESIGN LAB
GRAPHIC DESIGN STUDIO

KNOWLEDGE MANAGEMENT CENTER
WATER COOLER
WASHROOM

Locational Hnaging Signs

AQUARIUM
AMPHITHEATER
BOARD ROOM 1-2

Testing: Cone Of Vision

Forms for Sign Boards

Directional Signs

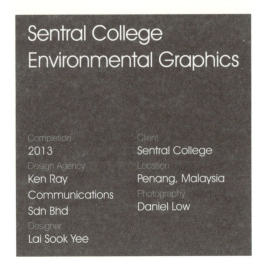

Sentral College
Environmental Graphics

Completion
2013
Design Agency
Ken Ray
Communications
Sdn Bhd
Designer
Lai Sook Yee

Client
Sentral College
Location
Penang, Malaysia
Photography
Daniel Low

In the mix of a rebranding exercise there was the development of the college's environmental graphics that is bold, colourful and eye-catching. Big 3D floor numbering and directional signage greet visitors. Each floor is also colour coded for differentiation. These way-finders are designed to attract attention and provide clear directional guide for visitors and students to navigate around the campus. The stylish wraparound arrows along corridors are both functional and attractive with highly legible font for distinct information. The result is a functional yet aesthetically pleasing design that has now become part of the college's identity.

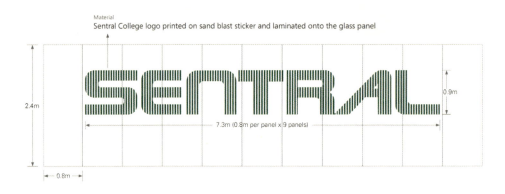

Material
Sentral College logo printed on sand blast sticker and laminated onto the glass panel

2.4m

0.9m

7.3m (0.8m per panel x 9 panels)

0.8m

46cm

Spray painted on wooden plank

Depth
2.54cm

**LR
9.02
–
9.11**

Theatre Room I

Font Type
Segoe Semibold
Regular

Material
Colour Sticker

46cm

50cm

**LR
9.12
–
9.14**

1.2m

Spray painted on wooden plank

Depth
5.08cm

1.2m

7

LEVEL 7

**Online
Computer
Rooms**
OCR 1 - 5

IT Office

**Student Affairs
& Services
Department**

Board Room

**Club Meeting
Room**

**Rest and
Recuperate Room**

Font Type
Segoe Semibold
Regular

Font Type
Segoe Bold

Material
Colour Sticker

Depth
2.54cm

1.2m

9

LEVEL 9

**Lecture
Rooms**
LR 9.01 - 9.14

Theatre Room I

1m

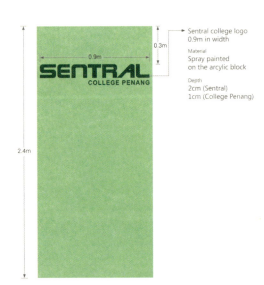

Sentral college logo
0.9m in width

Material
Spray painted
on the arcylic block

Depth
2cm (Sentral)
1cm (College Penang)

0.3m

0.9m

2.4m

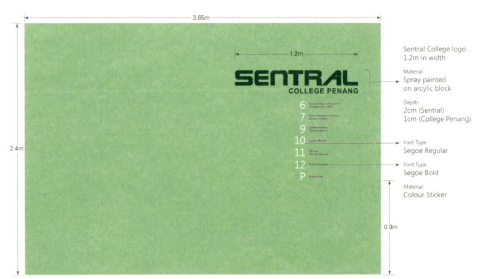

3.65m

Sentral College logo
1.2m in width

Material
Spray painted
on arcylic block

Depth
2cm (Sentral)
1cm (College Penang)

Font Type
Segoe Regular

Font Type
Segoe Bold

Material
Colour Sticker

1.2m

2.4m

0.9m

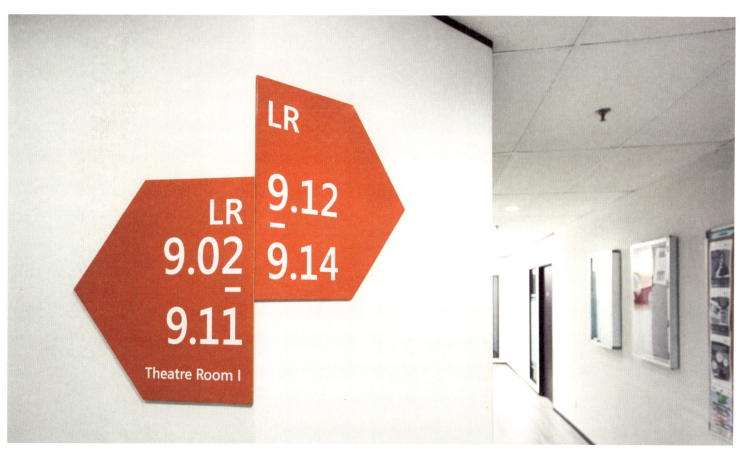

Wayfinding Project at RIT

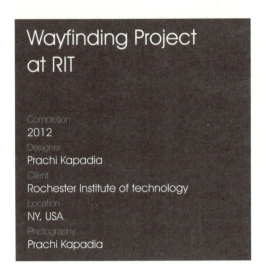

Completion
2012
Designer
Prachi Kapadia
Client
Rochester Institute of technology
Location
NY, USA
Photography
Prachi Kapadia

The wayfinding study project is a proposed design project with a new navigational signage system that highlights ease of navigation, good quality design, maintaining the colour palette throughout exterior and Interior signage, informative and functional signage. It reflects simplicity and easily communicates to the audience than the old signage system.

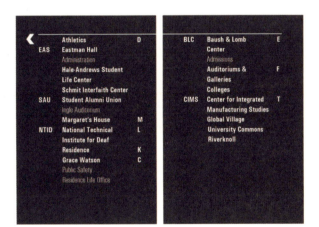

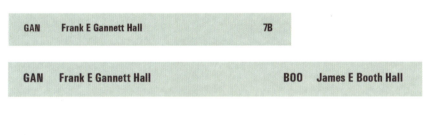

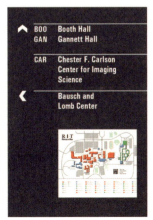

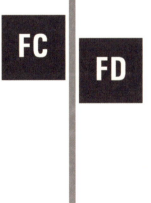

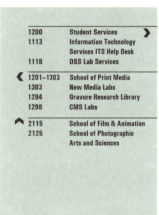

Wayfinding System for the French National Archives

Completion
2014

Design Agency
Intégral Ruedi Baur

Designers
Ruedi Baur,
Stéphanie Brabant,
Simon Burkhart, Eva
Kubinyi

Client
French Ministry
of Culture and
Communication

Location
Paris, France

Photography
Chloé Gassian

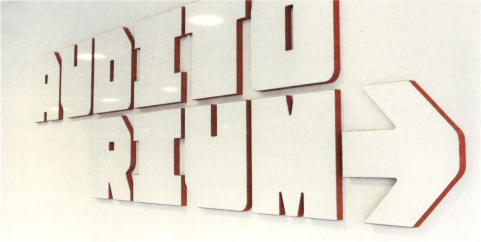

The customised typeface designed for the visual identity of the Archives is based on the idea of accumulation and storage. Conceived for bidimensiond and tridimensional use, it is applied to the wayfinding so as to identify the buildings primary structure and main functions. Designed from square shapes, the letters make up a virtual grid system which allows arrangement of text and media. Outside the building the letters are designed as self-supporting cubes made of coloured concrete. In the spaces open to the public, the letters become "flatter" until they loose all volume in the storage areas and are painted directly onto the walls. The letters use plywood for the inside, to make brilliant surfaces contrast with matt colored wooden edges.

Salle de lecture
Inventaires
Microfilms

Le centre
des Archives nationales
de Pierrefitte-sur-Seine
a été inauguré par

Monsieur François Hollande
président de la République

le 11 février 2013

L'association des amis des Archives
de France fait don de cette plaque intégrée
aux Archives nationales

Madame Doriana Fuksas
Monsieur Massimiliano Fuk
Architectes

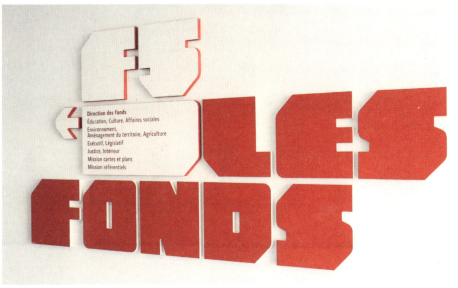

Direction des fonds
Éducation, Culture, Affaires sociales
Environnement,
Aménagement du territoire, Agriculture
Exécutif, Législatif
Justice, Intérieur
Mission cartes et plans
Mission référentiels

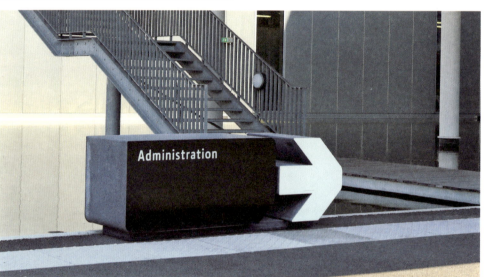

Library of the University of Münster

Completion
2011
Design Agency
Nowakteufelknyrim
Designers
Stefan Nowak,
Dominik Mycielski,
Buero211, Bärbel
Maxisch

Client
Universitätsbibliothek
Münster
Location
Münster, Germany
Photography
Stefan Nowak,
Dominik Mycielski

At the beginning of a control system is a white wall. The control system of the university library Munster waived metope or signs. Instead, on-site areas are used to place the information. For each user of the university library of Munster, it is important that he "understands" the building: The floor signs are structured so that the information is easy to read and be detected quickly in spite of its density. The return centre is carried out on existing wall surfaces along the lines of sight of the main traffic routes. The intentionally large-sized lettering is already clearly visible from a distance.

← Internet-Arbeitsplätze
   Fernleihe

→

Publikations-Service

Hospital Mater Dei
Signage System

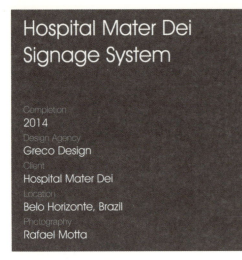

Completion
2014
Design Agency
Greco Design
Client
Hospital Mater Dei
Location
Belo Horizonte, Brazil
Photography
Rafael Motta

This wayfinding system was designed for Mater Dei Hospital. In dealing with a large-sized building, which may undergo future alterations in its internal flow, a modular signage system makes the exchange of information easier, while furnishing integrity to the system as a whole. Mater Dei's symbol, a cross made with injection molded ABS plastic, is the main linking point between all the equipment pieces. The pictograms, whose designs follow the elements of Myriad – the logo's typography, deliver even greater singularity and identity to the project.

Código Amarelo
Ligue 9998

Código Azul
Ligue 9191

Acesso Restrito
Restricted Access

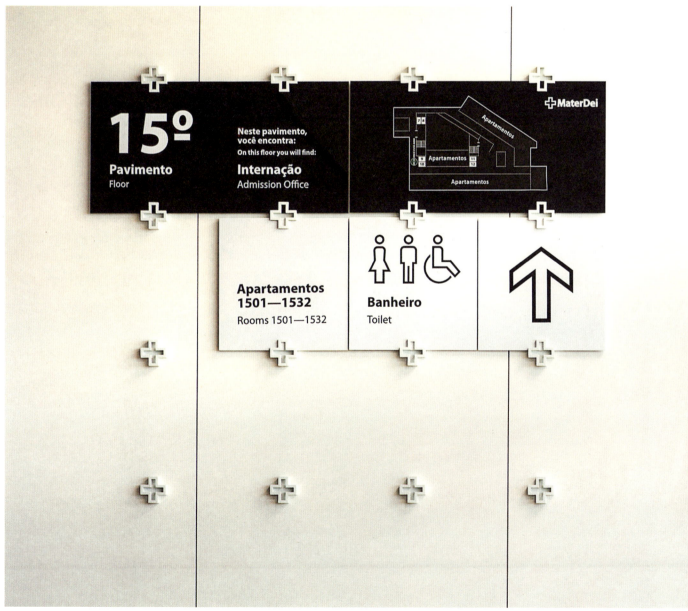

15º
Pavimento
Floor

Neste pavimento,
você encontra:
On this floor you will find:
Internação
Admission Office

Apartamentos
1501—1532
Rooms 1501—1532

Banheiro
Toilet

MaterDei

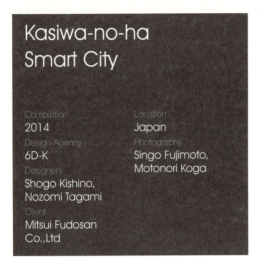

Kasiwa-no-ha
Smart City

Completion
2014
Design Agency
6D-K
Designers
Shogo Kishino,
Nozomi Tagami
Client
Mitsui Fudosan
Co.,Ltd

Location
Japan
Photography
Singo Fujimoto,
Motonori Koga

The development projects of Mitsui real estate are divided into two parts: business hotels and exhibition facilities, apartments and residences. For the fact that people do not often visit the areas of the apartments and residences, the information requires balance rather than strong expressiveness. In the intersection places where people live in, they used of the benches to mark branch points, so the destination is very clear.

The reason for using the benches as the branch points is that it is not a place where people often stay and gather. Therefore the information on the benches will be blocked when people sit on it, and will not be excessive leaked on the contrary. The designer thinks this design expresses good balance of the information.

The areas of business, universities, hotels, etc. are the places for a large number of researchers from other countries, so it uses multi-lingual labels and adds pictographic icons for easy understanding.

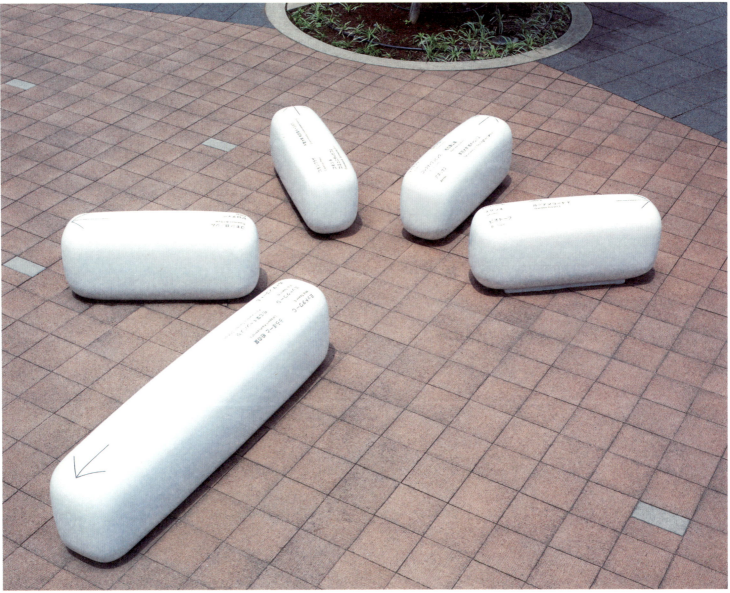

Hospital Signage System

Completion
2014
Designer
Ghadeer Abdulmohsen al-Oufi
Location
KSA, Jeddah

The designer thought of having a unique theme for the signage system of a hospital, and made it calm and optimistic for patients. The designer used wood material, which reveals stress.

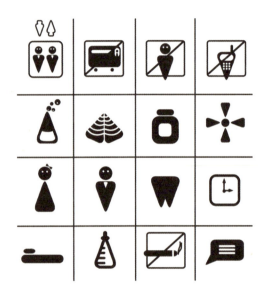

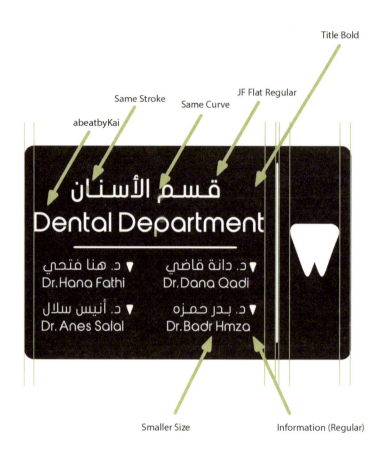

Title Bold

JF Flat Regular

Same Curve

Same Stroke

abeatbyKai

قسم الأسنان
Dental Department

▾ د. هنا فتحي   ▾ د. دانة قاضي
Dr.Hana Fathi   Dr.Dana Qadi

▾ د. أنيس سلال   ▾ د. بدر حمزه
Dr.Anes Salal   Dr.Badr Hmza

Smaller Size

Information (Regular)

حمام نساء
Female Toilet

الإستعلامات
Information

دكتورة أطفال
Pediatrics
د. غدير العوفي
Dr.Ghadeer Alofi

المختبر
Laboratory

حمام رجال
Male Toilet

قسم الأسنان
Dental Department

مخرج
Exit

أشعة تحت الإستخدام
X-Ray In Use

المختبر
Laboratory

ممنوع استخدام الجوال
No Mobile Phones

 حمامات الرجال والنساء
Male/Female Toilet

الصيدلية
Pharmacy

المختبر
Laboratory

الأشعة
X-Ray

أوقات الزيارة
Visiting Hours

كل يوم من الساعة 4 عصرا - 10مساء
Every day From 4 P.M – 10 P.M

 مصعد
Elevator

ممنوع التدخين
No Smoking

قسم الأسنان
Dental Department

▼ د. هنا فتحي   ▼ د. دانة قاضي
Dr.Hana Fathi   Dr.Dana Qadi

▼ د. أنيس سلال   ▼ بدر حمزه
Dr. Anes Salal   Dr.Badr Hmza

الصيدلية
Pharmacy

الدور
Floor

المختبر
Laboratory

2

الأشعة
X-Ray

غرف المرضى
Patient's Room
75–80

Wayfinding System for the Silesian Hospital in Cieszyn

Completion
2013

Designer
Iwona Przybyła

Location
Cieszyn, Poland

Photography
Iwona Przybyła

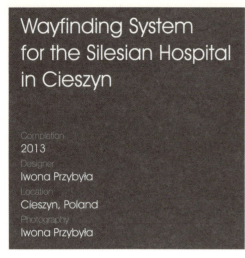

The proposed design of the new wayfinding system for the Silesian Hospital in Cieszyn was based on the analysis of the current system. The aim of the project was to develop a new, consistent set of markings which would make use of many solutions used currently and the habits of the personnel, but re-organise many elements in order to optimize the way people move around the facility.

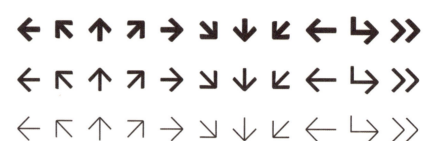

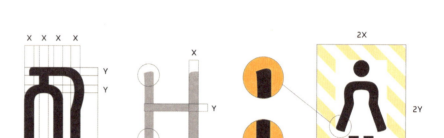

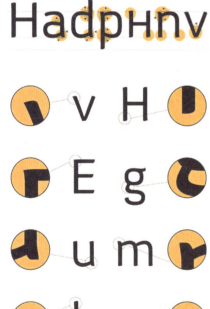

The project consists of two major stages. The aim of the first stage was the creation of an appropriate font style. Two variants, regular and light, were designed for the purpose of this project. The goal of the second stage was to design a set of pictograms and arrows necessary to describe key places in the facility.

Finally, the elements designed during the course of the project were used to create sample boards showcasing the potential use of the wayfinding system at the Silesian Hospital.

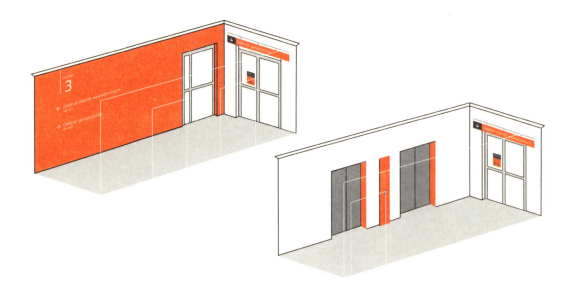

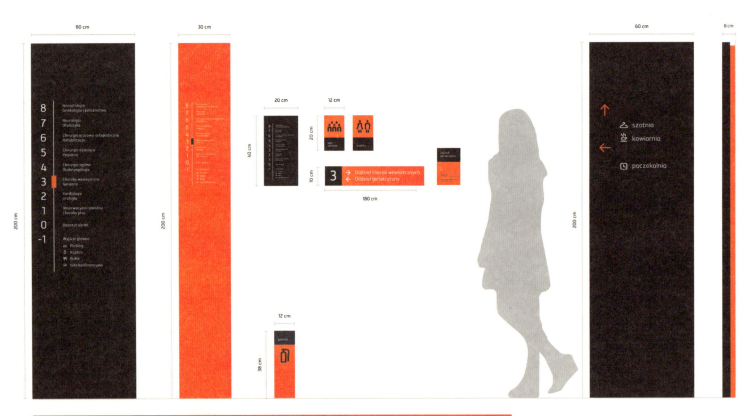

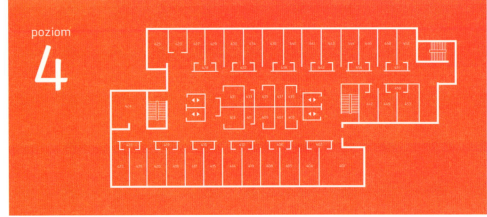

Oasi-Wayfinding

Completion
2014

Designers
Riccardo Gioria, Alessandro Michelazzo,
Erica Zipoli

Client
University of Venice-Master class at IUAV
Ospedale San Giovanni e Paolo

Location
Venice, Italy

The goal of the project is to concretely express the reality of the oasis which is protected from the stress of the city. Indeed, the only thing that the user does in the hospital is to take care of himself / herself. Part of this project is to include the courtyard and the green areas within the identity of the hospital as fundamental part of the experience of the user. The signage system is partly related to this approach because it reflects the metaphor of ecosystem.

They specifically designed a set of pictograms to be adapted to the typeface they chose and a couple of patterns to identify the two areas of the hospital.

The project was carried to create specific installations in each courtyard of the hospital, to attract the user to stop for a while to contemplate the nature.

They also decided to include some natural wooden details within the signage system to suggest a warmer and more comfortable atmosphere, a supplement which keeps unchanged the typical signage system of the hospital made of simplicity and accuracy; however, it relieves the emotional impact tied to the fragile reality of the hospital.

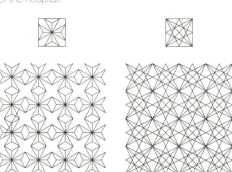

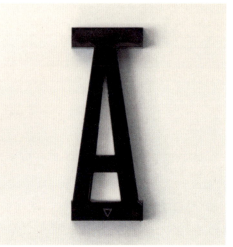

De Locomotief, Rehabilitation Centre for Children

Completion
2013
Design Agency
MMOS
Designers
Frea Mathijssen, Eveline Meijering
Location
Belgium
Photography
Sander Muylaert

The need of flexibility in 'De Locomotief', comes from a continuous change of function of the different therapy rooms.

The result is a black and white design which is used throughout the entire building. At the entrance you will find a structured overview of all the therapy rooms and available therapists with an assigned symbol. These symbols are found throughout the building on the corresponding door of the therapy room.

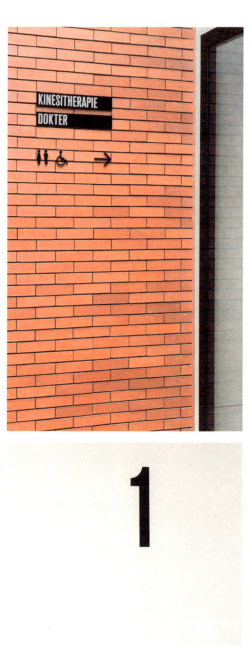

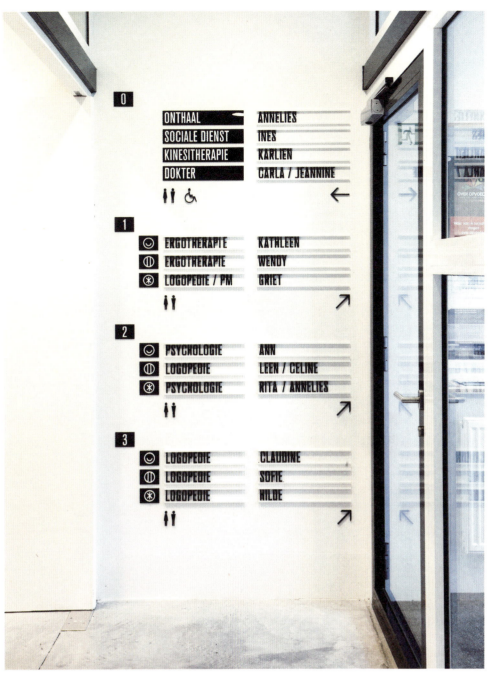

The acrylic signage is applied directly to the walls and doors. The flexible part of the signage consists of separate letters. These letters can be slid between the aluminum profiles attached to the wall. This provides the necessary flexibility.

A clear type is used in combination with abstract symbols. The colour choice is based on the existing architecture where black and white are predominantly used. This communicates clearly to the parents and staff as well as to the children. The result is an aesthetically pleasing and well functioning, effective signage.

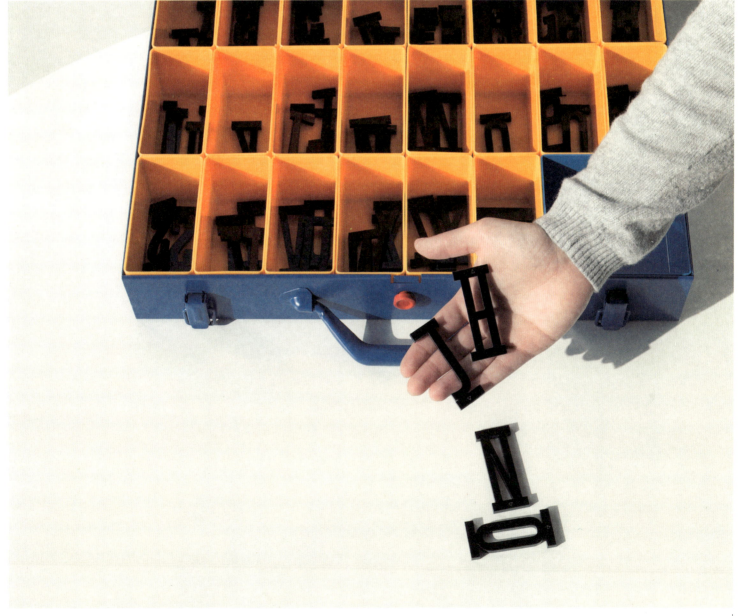

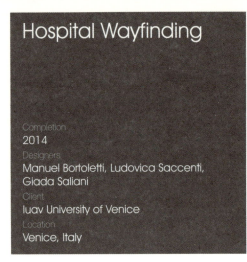

Hospital Wayfinding

Completion
2014
Designers
Manuel Bortoletti, Ludovica Saccenti,
Giada Saliani
Client
Iuav University of Venice
Location
Venice, Italy

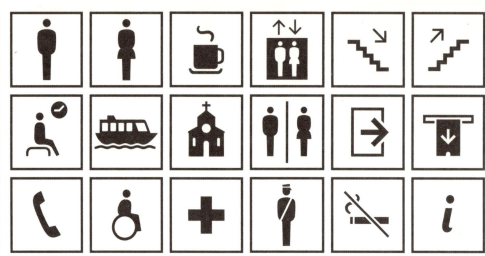

This project takes as target the creation of a wayfinding system for SS. Giovanni e Paolo hospital in Venice. From the architectural point of view the structure presents unique and characterised different styles from different eras.

The entire hospital complex is developed in such a way that it seems almost a sort of archipelago in which each pavilion represents an island.

The concept is developed from this suggestion which goes around that navigation metaphor and it is strongly tied to the theme of wayfinding.

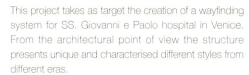

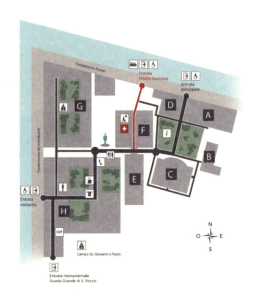

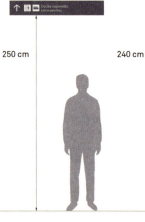

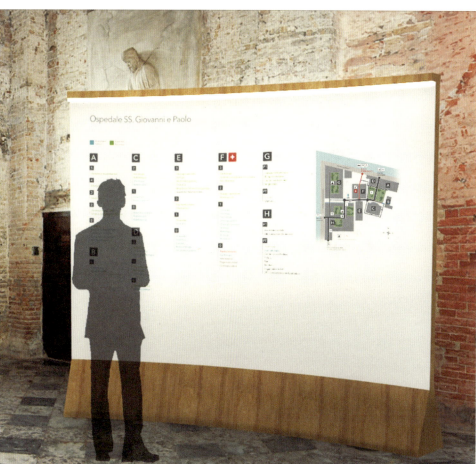

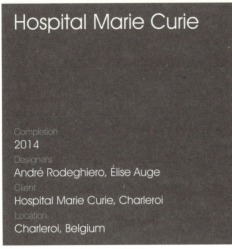

Hospital Marie Curie

Completion
2014
Designers
André Rodeghiero, Élise Auge
Client
Hospital Marie Curie, Charleroi
Location
Charleroi, Belgium

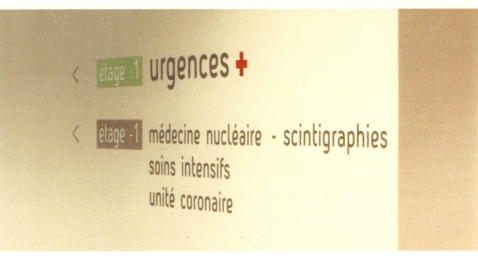

This hospital signage provides different perspectives for users such as patients, medical staff and visitors. In addition to the orientation function (name of places, easier flows and reassurance), this project developed specific environments making them human through the colour choices and the creation of an illustrative family.

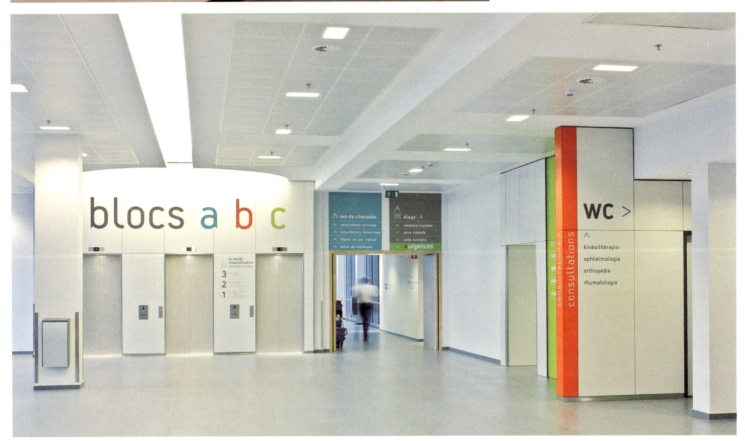

bloc.e

pediatrie

∧ rez-de-chaussée

∧ consultations oncologie
∧ consultations hématologie
∧ hôpital de jour médical
∧ salles de conférence

étage -1

∨ médecine nucléaire
∨ soins intensifs
∨ unité coronaire
∨ +urgences

< bloc a hôpital de jour médical
< bloc a salles de conférence

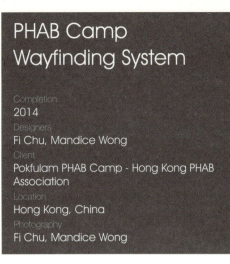

PHAB Camp
Wayfinding System

Completion
2014
Designers
Fi Chu, Mandice Wong
Client
Pokfulam PHAB Camp - Hong Kong PHAB
Association
Location
Hong Kong, China
Photography
Fi Chu, Mandice Wong

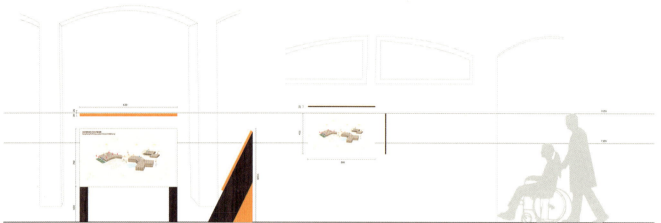

Orientation Sign - Ground Planted

Orientation Sign - Wall Mounted

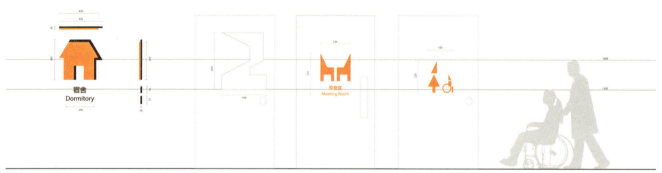

Identification Sign - Wall Mounted

Identification Sign - Wall Painted

Directional Sign - Ground Planted

Directional Sign - Wall Painted

Information Sign - Wall Mounted

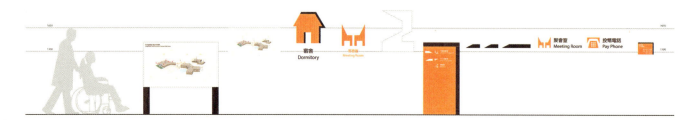

PHAB Camp is a camp site which is free access for the disabled. Therefore the signage must have a thoughtful consideration for them, height, size etc. So do the concept built, 'Acceptance'. Geometric shapes were applied. Single shape has limited diversification, unless shapes grouped and formed. Likewise, stronger power appears when people accept and help each other.

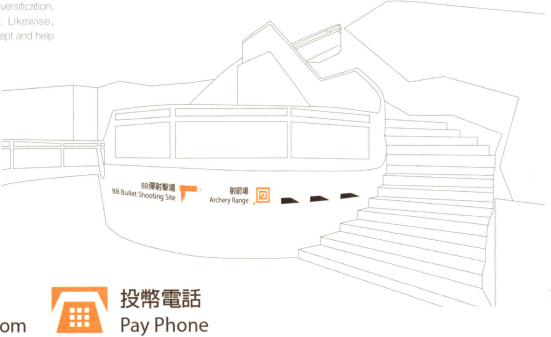

聚會室
Meeting Room

投幣電話
Pay Phone

Copernicus Science Centre

Completion
2010
Designers
Mamastudio and Piotr Stolarski
Client
Copernicus Science Center,
Warsaw, Poland
Location
Warsaw, Poland

The Copernicus Science Centre wayfinding system was designed to highlight the building's architecture and surroundings in a subtle but clear way. The designers' task was to create a unique system that would immediately create associations with structure. The characteristic form of the building was used by Mamastudio as a source of inspiration. Irregular forms visible on architectural plans have been repeated in the shape of information modules, signs and icons. The typography repeats the shapes and rhythm of the icons to ensure further consistency. Associations with the Centre were additionally enhanced by the usage of colours presented in the institution's identification system.

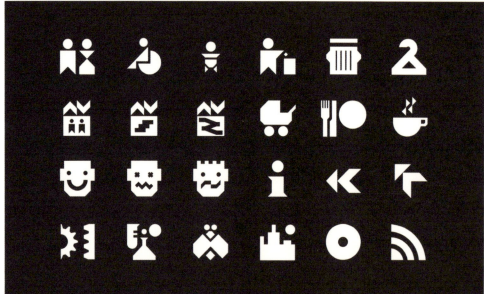

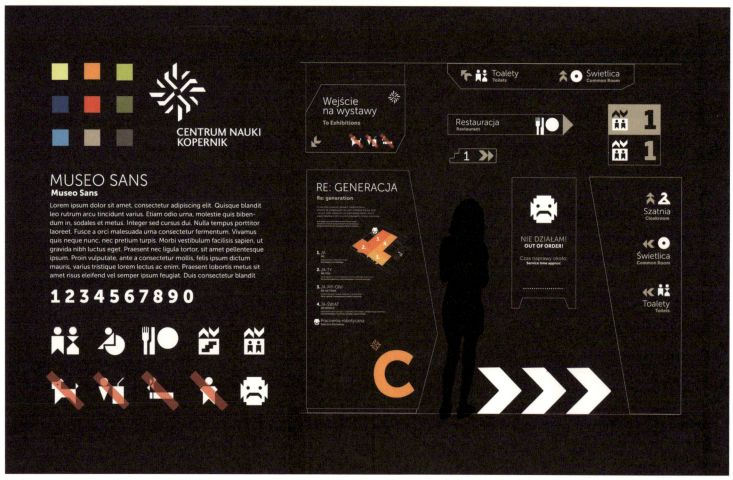

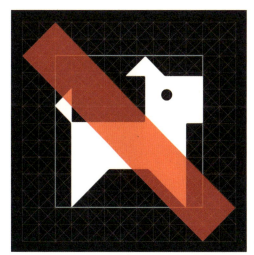

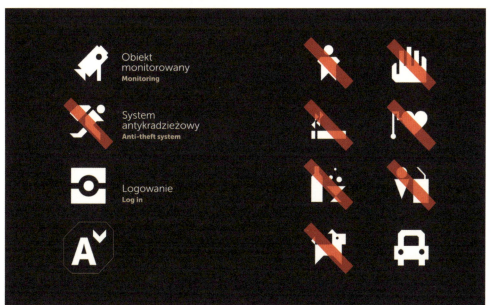

	Obiekt **monitorowany** Monitoring	
	System **antykradzieżowy** Anti-theft system	
	Logowanie Log in	

The Copernicus Science Centre in Warsaw is built on an open plan which means there are a few walls on which signage could be placed. Mamastudio's solution was to create special three-dimensional and free-standing forms of whose shapes are inspired by the architecture and which are used as a source of direction. Maps and plans placed on the blocks help visitors find their way. Minimal use of colours, simplicity and consistency of design ensured visibility on the multi-colured background of numerous exhibitions and often changed exhibits.

The system is intuitive and easily navigable, noticeable in two languages (Polish and English) and clearly recognisable without being overwhelming or driving attention away from the exhibition.

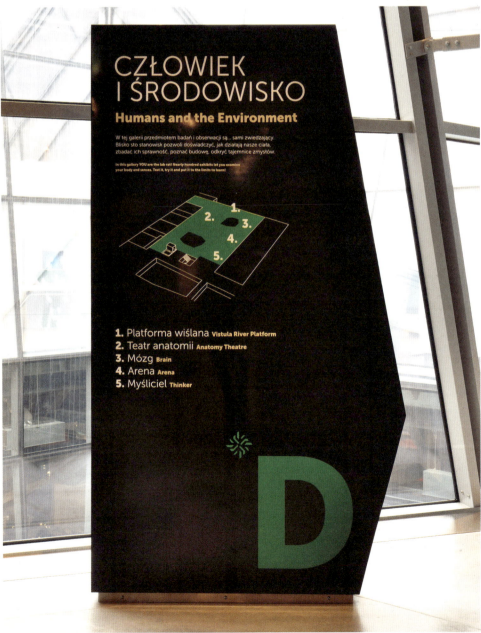

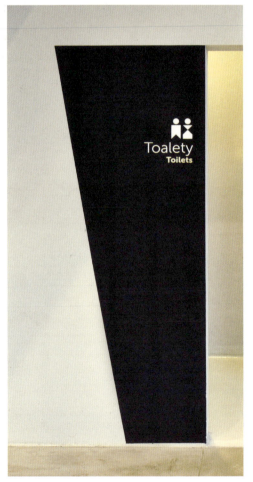

Centro Cultural de Belém

Completion
2014
Designer
Martina Cocco
Location
Lisbon, Portugal
Photography
Martina Cocco

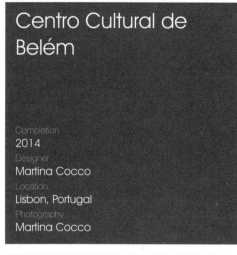

The project is carried to develop a signage system, and also to rebrand for the Centro Cultural de Belém in Lisbon, Portugal. The wayfinding system of the centre was designed to highlight the building's architecture and surroundings in a subtle, but clear manner. The aim of the indoor signage system is to enhances the architecture of the building and lead the experience through the Centre. The pictograms were designed from the logo with variations in thickness, fullness and emptiness. All the pictograms are inscribed in regular squared modules.

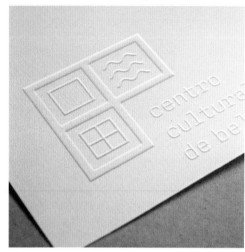

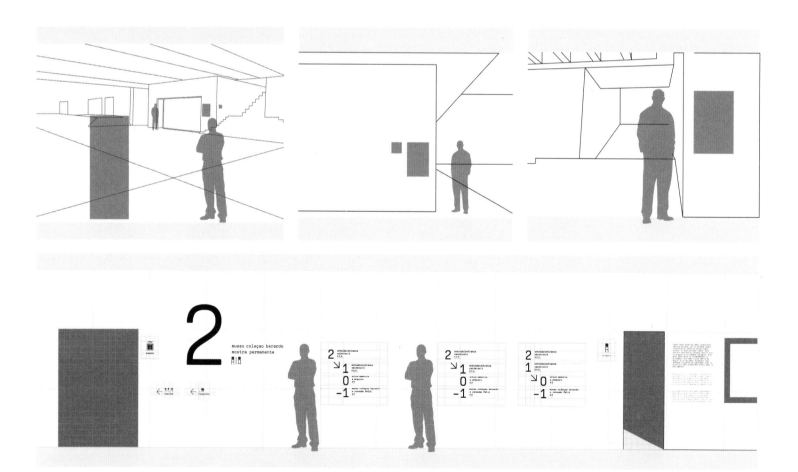

The font in use for this project is Excellent, a monospaced font by Lineto. This geometric, edgy and geometric font, is well-suited to the whole wayfinding system.

museo coleção berardo
mostra permanente

2 entrada|entrance
  saída|exit

1 entrada|entrance
  saída|exit

0 entre memória
  e arquivo

-1 museo coleção berardo
   o consumo feliz

← toalete

← reception

Egon Schiele (Tulln an der Donau,
12 de Junho de 1890–Viena, 31
de Outubro de 1918) foi um pintor
austríaco ligado ao movimento
expressionista.

Egon Schiele (June 12, 1890 – October
31, 1918) was an Austrian painter.
Schiele was a major figurative painter
of the early 20th century and an early
exponent of Expressionism.

The signage system was developed in two parts: the outdoor signage is composed of a vertical panel with the complete mapping of the building, the signs indicating how to get to the main rooms of the Centre and the signs with only pictograms, placed nearby the places to which they relate. Differently the indoor signage is always applied directly on the walls, by adhesive prints or ink. The aim of the indoor signage system is to enhances the architecture of the building and leads the experience through the Centre. The final result is a space with a intuitive and easily navigable wayfinding system..

125 Years of Fernando Pessoa

Completion
2014
Designer
Ana Cláudia Oliveira
Location
Lisbon, Portugal
Photography
Ana Cláudia Oliveira

This is an event inspired by the multiplicity of the Portuguese poet Fernando Pessoa. It consists in five itineraries in Lisbon, corresponding to each of his five heteronyms. The identity enhances the concept of plurality through the letter S that resembles the glasses of Fernando Pessoa alluding to his five visions. The wayfinding system, which was designed for the cultural centre Casa Fernando Pessoa, discloses the idea of self-fragmentation through the pictograms composed of a base (red) and fragments in relief (black) creating dynamic and visual rhythm when combined with sign boards in folded paper shape.

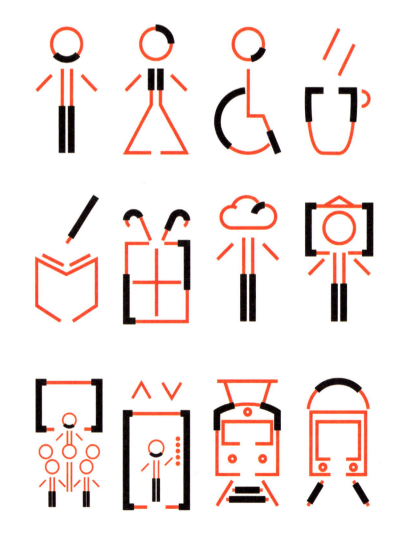

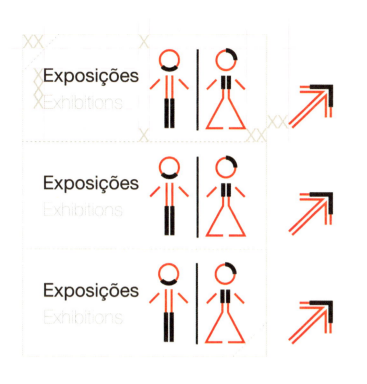

Exposições
Exhibitions

Exposições
Exhibitions

Exposições
Exhibitions

Exposições
Exhibitions

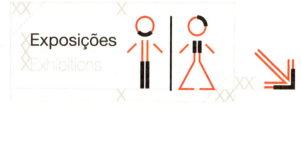

Exposições
Exhibitions

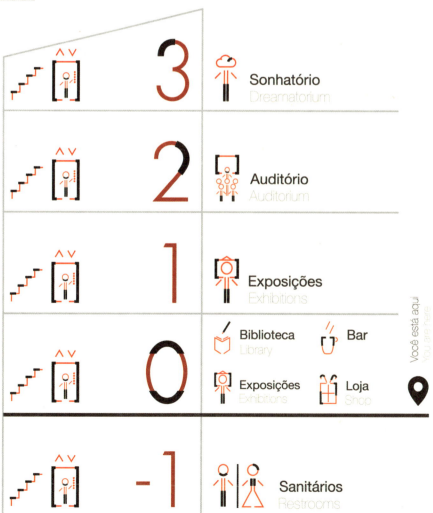

3 Sonhatório
Dreamatorium

2 Auditório
Auditorium

1 Exposições
Exhibitions

0

Biblioteca
Library

Bar

Exposições
Exhibitions

Loja
Shop

Você está aqui
You are here

-1 Sanitários
Restrooms

Une Gamme

Completion
2014
Design Agency
Intégral Ruedi Baur
Designers
Ruedi Baur, David Thoumazeau, Matthieu Thonnard, Eva Kubinyi

Client
EO Guidage Company
Location
Paris, France
Photography
Intégral Ruedi Baur

This ongoing project development was presented to the CNIT Exhibition Urbaccess of Paris – La Défense. Intégral Ruedi Baur developed new aesthetic and technical solutions to facilitate access of the city to the greatest number according to EO Guidage requirements. The multi sensory signage system allows for a comprehensive and coherent response to various scenarios one may find in a city, from a public building to a transport terminal.

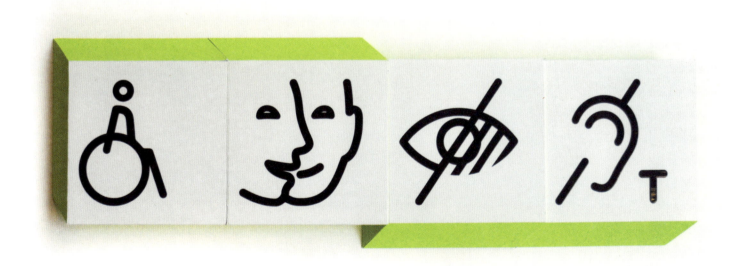

197

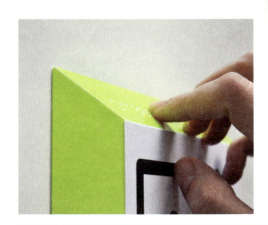

Tipos Latinos Signage System

Completion
2012
Design Agency
Estudio FABULA
Client
Tipos Latinos Argentina
Location
Buenos Aires, Argentina
Photography
Jean Catalano & Agustina García

The goal of this project was to make a 100% recycle signage system with a high end quality. This system was used for Tipos Latinos, the most important typography biennial in Latin America.

The designers thought the entire design process: from the concept and the graphic design of each sign to the production with recyclable cardboard and water based inks. These projects show they can make great products with a very low environment impact.

móviles en el siglo XXI
Making Faces: Metal Type in the
21st Century, de Richard Kegler
(Estados Unidos/2011)

| Jue | 10 | 18:30 | Taller | CCEBA P | @ |

Modulografía (tipografía modular) II
Fernanda Cozzi, Sebastián Gagin
y Guillermo Vizzari

| Sáb | 12 | 11:00 | Visita guiada | CCEBA P | |

| Lun | 14 | 19:00 | Inauguración | UCES | |

Edward Johnston, letras con vida

| Mié | 16 | 18:30 | Conferencia | CCEBA P | |

**Tipografía colonial porteña:
de 1780 a 1810**
Fabio Ares

| Jue | 17 | 11:00 | Demostración de caligrafía | UCES | |

Caligrafía en acción
Maria Eugenia Roballos y Betina Naab

| | | 18:00 | Demostración de letterpress | IDEAL | @ |

Entre tinta y máquinas
Patricio Gatti

| Sáb | 19 | 11:00 | Visita guiada | CCEBA P | |
| | | 16:00 | Conferencia | CCEBA P | |

Tipografía con razón de ser
Charlie Zinno

Edward Johnston, letras con vida | UCES

| Lun | 21 | 18:30 | Demostración de caligrafía | | |

Caligrafía en acción
Maria Eugenia Roballos y Betina Naab | CCEBA P

| Mar | 22 | 19:00 | Mesa redonda | | |

De la universidad a la P...

CCEBA P

da | UCES

Tipos Latinos 2012
Quinta Bienal de Tipografía
Latinoamericana

Sedes
Buenos Aires, Córdoba, Mendoza, Paraná,
Posadas, Santa Fe, San Juan, Cochabamba,
La Paz, Santa Cruz de la Sierra, Recife,
Río de Janeiro, São Paulo, Santiago,
Bogotá, La Habana, Cuenca, Guayaquil, Loja
Quito, Guatemala, México, San Luis Potosí,
Tijuana, Veracruz, Asunción, Lima,
Montevideo, Caracas, El Cairo, Berlín,
Bucarest, Manila, Manchester, Valencia
y son cada vez más.

Penguin Parade Visitor Centre

Completion	Client
2013	Phillip Island Nature
Design Agency	Parks
Crampton d+a,	Location
Bohn Studio	Phillip Island,
Designers	Australia
David Crampton,	Photography
Andie Froutzis	Peter Bennetts

Inspired by the waddling, pint-sized stars of this world-famous tourist destination, Crampton d+a and Bohn Studio re-imagined the visitor journey to reflect the penguin's pre-dawn / post-sunset roundtrip from 'burrow to sea, and sea to burrow'; executing the concept in the main circulation spaces via a new, darker colour palette, significantly reduced light levels, and a series of fun, educational insertions that reveal the everyday experiences and encounters that a penguin may face. Not only did this bring the magic outside world of the penguin inside, it also engendered a more theatrical mood that heightened visitor anticipation for the experience to come.

Eco-friendly finishes predominated the material palette, particularly plywood, which was used as a unifying element across all insertions, signage and interpretive displays – an element that also underscored the attraction's conversation theme, and enabled cost savings because of its suitability for direct printing.

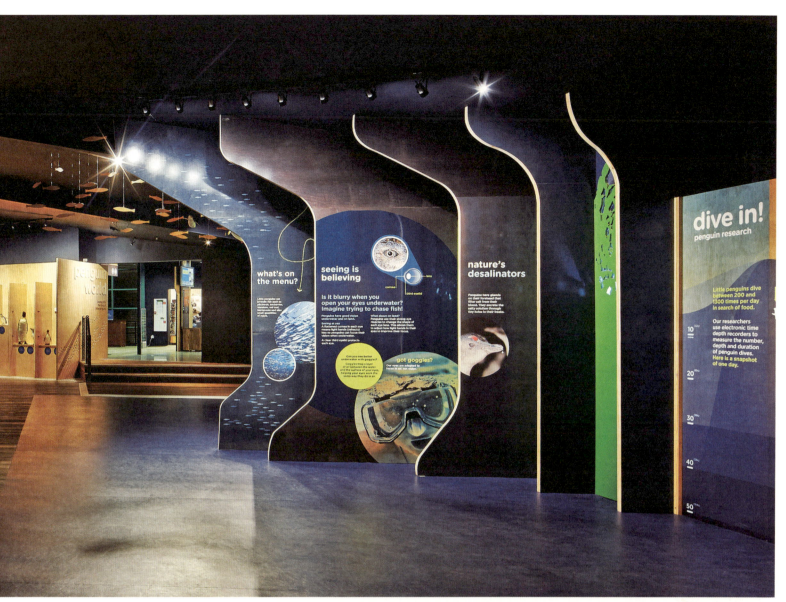

The Look and Feel for "Vendimia National Fest 2015"

Completion
2014
Designer
Fernando Viñas – Valentina Candia
Client
Government of Mendoza, Argentina
Location
Mendoza, Argentina
Photography
Fernando Viñas

The Vendimia National Festival is the most important grape harvest celebration throughout Argentina. It consists of several happenings and events, which take place in different sites of the city and ultimately lead to the main act in the amphitheatre of Mendoza. The festival itself lasts only one week, but its promotion starts a couple of months prior to it, for that reason it is very important to generate a certain atmosphere and framework for the event.

City post sign

Amphitheatre general signage

Amphitheatre location

Amphitheatre access

In order to have a complete and strong corporate identity, the designer created a consequent graphic system, which consists of brand development, promotional posters, secondary elements and a signage system. Due to the fact that the majority of visitors are tourists, it was very crucial and necessary to offer a certain guidance through the wayfinding system. There are two different signage groups: to guide the people to the events they'd like to attend within and around the city; to help people find their seats and services inside the big amphitheatre to assure a kind of pleasant and comfortable experience.

The 21th International Symposium on Electronic Art

Completion
2014
Design Agency
SaySo Design
with CACE, Zayed
University
Designers
Nazima Ahmad,
Mariam Bin
Humaidan, Fatima
Hassan

Client
International
Symposium on
Electronic art
Location
Dubai, Abu Dhabi,
Sharjah

The design for ISEA 2014 is a generative process of capturing key elements of ISEA, which are innovation, science, electronics and art, while simultaneously painting a visual narrative of the United Arab Emirates (UAE). The UAE is a place that is constantly transforming but always maintaining its core values of cultural unity.

With the theme of location, ISEA 2014 is the power source for linking different areas around the UAE. Hence, the map of the UAE is seen as an electric grid. The designers first mapped the seven Emirates and identified the active and inactive locations. After that they created a physical link between the locations. This was then translated digitally to create infinite forms, expressing the vibrant but ever transforming nature of this unique location in the world.

The project involved branding and signage for multiple exhibitions, an academic conference, along with evening and day time events in 19 different locations around Dubai, Sharjah and AbuDhabi.

Seattle Design Festival Urban Wayfinding

Completion
2014
Designers
Evan Chakroff,
Setion Branko, Adrian
Mac Donald, Arlinda
Lalaj, Heather Bazille,
Jonathan Beech,
Noah Jeppson,
Cat Silva

Client
Seattle Design
Festival
Location
Washington, USA
Photography
Noah Jeppson

Utilizing bicycle infrastructure, urban wayfinding signs reached out into surrounding neighborhood to direct citizens of Seattle towards the 2014 Seattle Design Festival Block Party. Laser cut oil board panels with laminated fluorescent paper were chosen to provide an economical solution that appeared organic and purposeful in nature. Neighborhood landmarks were boldly highlighted on an etched map illustrating a route; on the reverse side distances were indicated for pedestrian, transit, and bicycle travel time. The signs brought awareness to the event while providing a renewed sense of place and – temporarily affixed to bicycle racks – fit the "Design in Motion" theme.

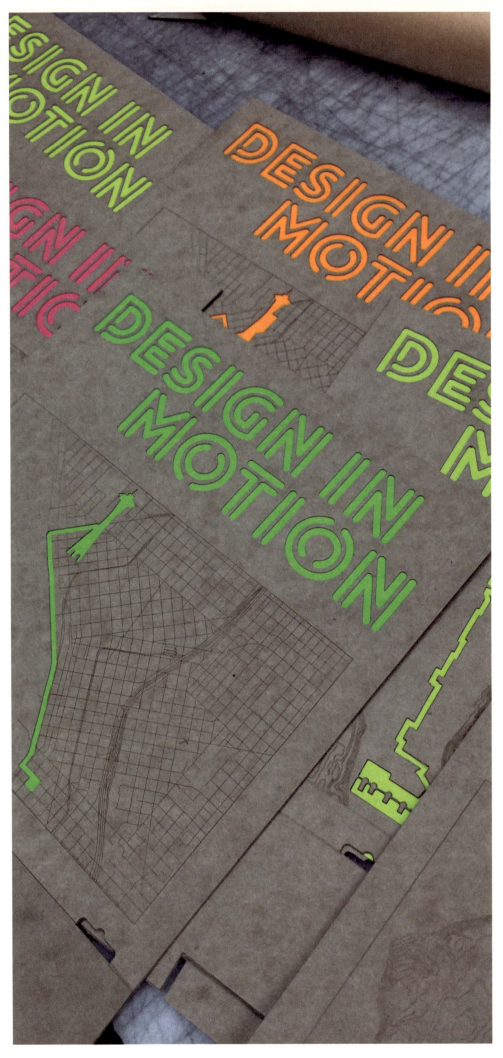

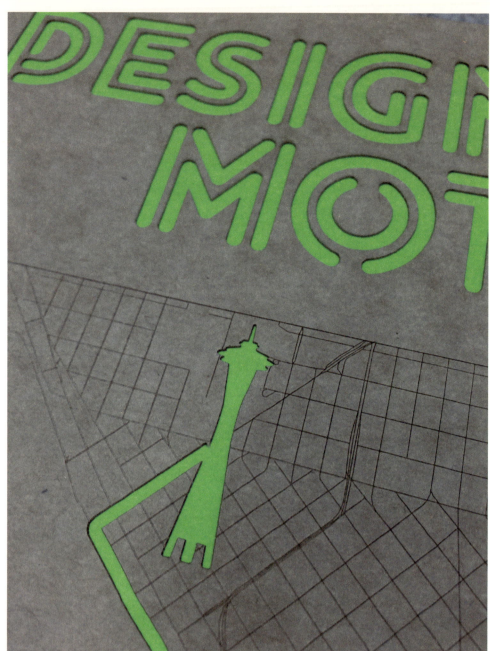

MCEC

Design Agency
R-Co Brand Identity
Designers
**Richard Henderson, Riesa Renata,
Damian McGrath, Mauris Lai**
Client
**Melbourne Convention
and Exhibition Centre**
Location
Australia
Photography
Jean-Marc La-Roque

The new Melbourne Convention and Exhibition Centre (MCEC) is an extraordinary architectural statement and the first '6 Star Green Star' environmentally rated convention centre in the world and the largest and most versatile convention and exhibition space in Southern Hemisphere. To provide a clear identification of its purpose, an identity and signage implementation program were required. Understanding the human dynamic, the signage response was to make the journey experience rewarding, bringing the essence of the MCEC brand to life through engaging directional and informational wayfinding.

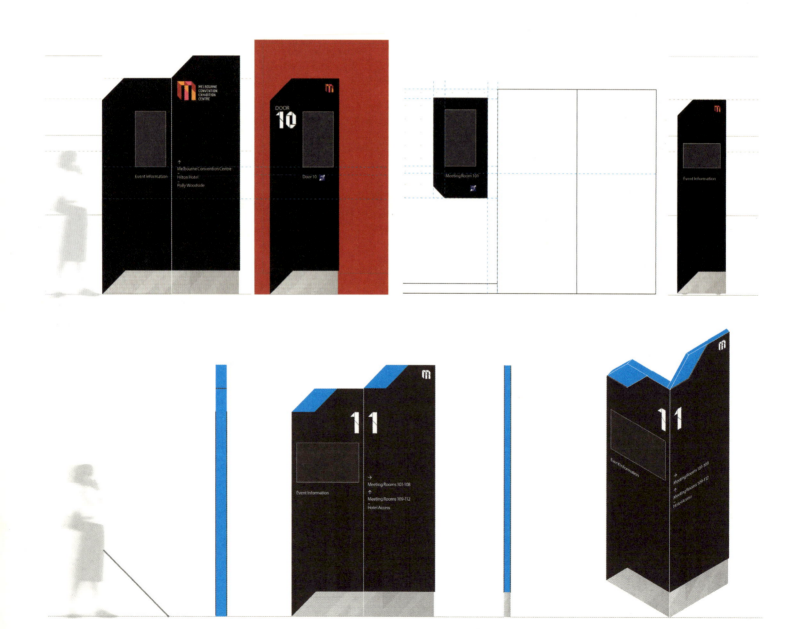

The brand for MCEC has been based upon one of the core attributes of the building – its ability to host a variety of activities (both large and small) and deliver an outstanding experience. In a competitive and congested global marketplace, the identity for the MCEC reinforces its positioning as 'Melbourne's Meeting Place'. The graphic 'M' symbolised both function and form, creating a striking and timeless reference point and visual language to its various collateral including signage and wayfinding. The graphic shapes created from this elegant visual pun are precise in their construction and content in their resolution. Each contact with signage provides an opportunity to engage with the brand and the architecture in a way that is meaningful and emotionally enriching.

Centro Cultural La Nau

Completion
2014
Designers
Ibán Ramón, DídacBallester
Client
Universitat de València
Location
Valencia, Spain
Photography
Ibán Ramón

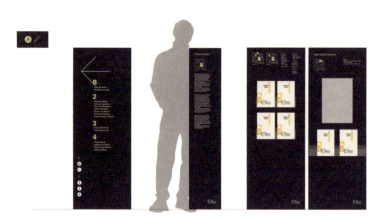

The new graphic solution escaped from historical approach of the previous project which preferred to demonstrate the presence and present a sober and functional appearance, but aesthetically it was separated from environment. Although some new specific elements were designed, reusing and adapting the existing elements was the most attractive part in this project.

Museum of Architecture Partial Refurbishment and Wayfinding System

Completion	Client
2014	Municipal Museum
Design Agency	of Architecture
ARCH_IT	Location
ARCHITECTURE+	Wrocław, Poland
DESIGN	Photography
Designers	Maciej Lulko
Piotr Zybura, Iga	
Peruga, Marian	
Misiak	

Low-cost, simple and clear wayfinding system is a core for partial refurbishment of existing post-bernardine building from XV century functioning as a Museum of Architecture (in polish: Muzeum Architektury) in Wroclaw, Poland. Elements of wayfinding system are essential for general architectural idea / solutions aimed to harmonise and link diverse areas of museum which – in lesser or greater extend – need renovation or reconstruction planned for the near future.

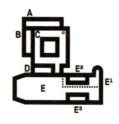

Font Makron

ABCDEFGHIJKLM
NOPQRSTUVWXYZ.
abcdefghijklnop
qrstuvwxyz.
1234567890!?[:]()

ABCDEFGHIJKLM
NOPQRSTUVWXYZ.
abcdefghijklnop
qrstuvwxyz.
1234567890!?[:]()

Pattern

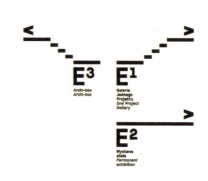

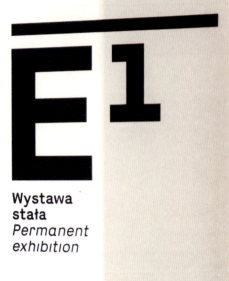

E1

Wystawa
stała
*Permanent
exhibition*

A **B**

Sala   Sala
Romańska Wschodnia
Romanes- *Eastern*
que Room *Room*

D/

Zakrystia
Sacristy

E1

Galeria
Jednego
Projektu
*One Project
Gallery*

E2

Wystawa
stała
*Permanent
exhibition*

▽ ○ ♿ Toaleta na
pierwszym piętrze
Toilets upstairs

⊟ ⬍ **A**

Sala
Romańska
*Romanesque
Room*

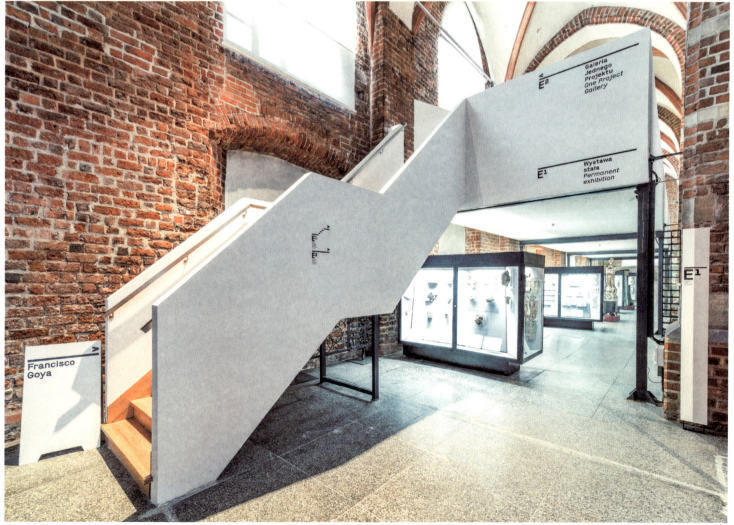

Francisco
Goya

E² Galeria
Jednego
Projektu
*One Project
Gallery*

E¹ Wystawa
stała
*Permanent
exhibition*

E¹

Signage Project for the Museum of Modern Art

Completion
2012
Designers
Luciano Ghysels, Yanina Castagnola,
Georgina Di Nenno
Client
Buenos Aires Museum of Modern Art
Location
Buenos Aires, Argentina
Photography
Luciano Ghysels, Yanina Castagnola

The communication strategy is mainly focused on making the museum as a dynamic museum, which becomes a part of the daily life of the people. It aims to achieve a link between art and user proposing "to be a part of the art". Dynamism and connection were the concepts on which this signage project was based. Diagonals and superposition were how the ideas were materialised. It was divided by colours depending on whether it was a permanent exhibition (green), temporary exhibition (magenta) or workshop (yellow). External signage was also thought to call the attention of the population.

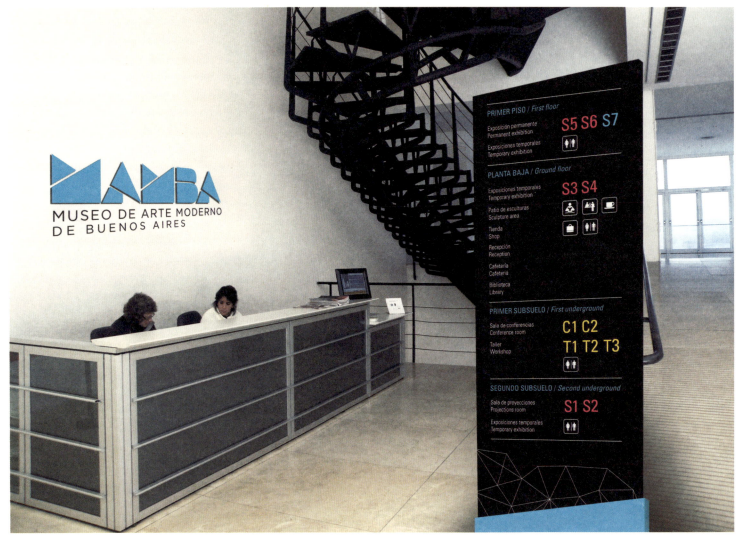

Wayfinding Project for 'Museu Blau'

Completion
2011

Location
Barcelona, Spain

Design Agency
Petit Comitè

Photography
Quim Massana,
Jordi Huaman

Designers
Quim Massana,
Yolanda Martin,
Jordi Huaman

Client
The Natural History
Museum of
Barcelona

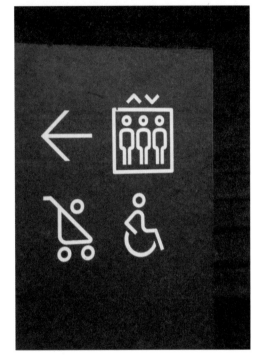

The project was done by the architects Herzog & DeMeuron, the designer of the building. The signs had to be discreet as not to interfere with the environment created by the architects. The result was simple, just a font in one color. The letters and icons in dark space were presented in a non-invasive way and its orderly arrangement improved orientation without sacrificing the expressiveness of space.

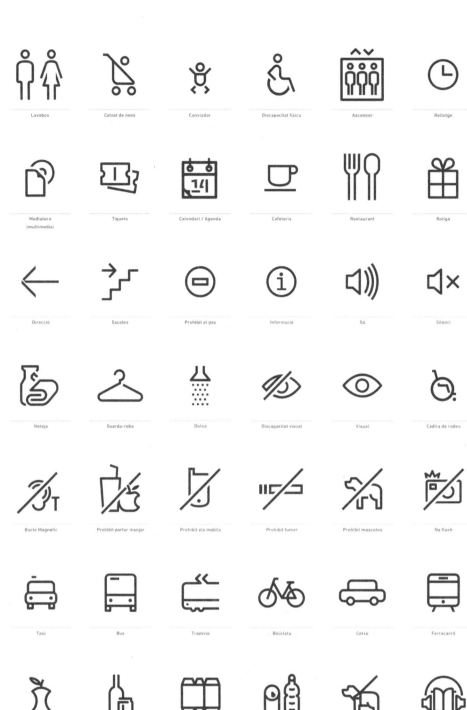

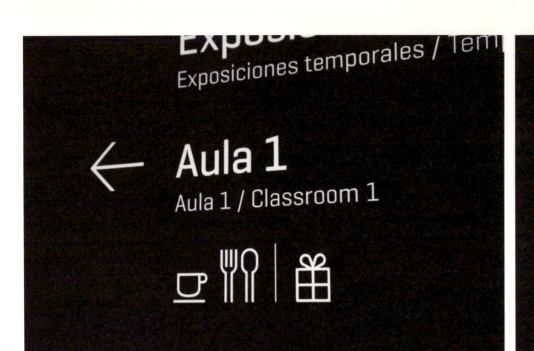

Exposi...
Exposiciones temporales / Tem...

← **Aula 1**
Aula 1 / Classroom 1

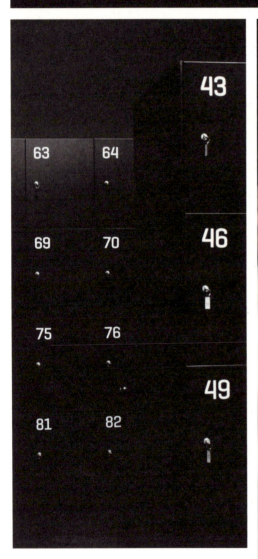

43

63 64

69 70

46

75 76

49

81 82

Informació i entrades →
Información y entradas / Information & tickets

Guarda-roba
Guardarropa / Cloakroom

Niu de ciència
Aula infantil / Aula infantil / Children's classroom

Aules 2 i 3
Aulas 2 y 3 / Classrooms 2 and 3

Sala d'actes
Salon de actos / Auditorium

Exposicions temporals
Exposiciones temporales / Temporary exhibitions

← **Aula 1**
Aula 1 / Classroom 1

Planeta vida →

Informació i entrades
Información y entradas / Information & tickets

Mediateca
Mediateca / Media library

Sortida
Salida / Exit

◤ **Entrada Museu**
Entrada Museo / Museum entrance

Informació i entrades →
Información y entradas / Information & tickets

Guarda-roba
Guardarropa / Cloakroom

Niu de ciència
Aula infantil / Aula infantil / Children's classroom

Aules 2 i 3
Aulas 2 y 3 / Classrooms 2 and 3

Sala d'actes
Salon de actos / Auditorium

Exposicions temporals
Exposiciones temporales / Temporary exhibitions

← **Aula 1**
Aula 1 / Classroom 1

Paseo del Bosque

Completion
2013
Designers
Colavita Ezequiel, Bibel Francisco, Bustos Mario
Location
Buenos Aires, Argentina

"Paseo del Bosque" is a green area located in La Plata City, Buenos Aires Province, Argentina, and the Natural Science Museum can be found inside its boundaries. This project was carried out academically, under the mentoring of the department of Arts of the National University of La Plata.

The goal was to create two wayfinding systems that could contribute to bringing a particular identity to the area, based on the mix of nature, human and industrial concepts. The system is made of sheets of plate and epoxy paint, and it will be arranged in the open air, pointing at entrances, tours and general interests spots. The second system, completed with translucent acrylic and vinyl, will be disposed to the interior of the museum, where it serves as a guide for each of the stages during a guided tour.

Berkshire Wayfinding System

Completion
2014
Designer
Markie Dossett
Location
Indiana, USA
Photography
Markie Dossett

This is a project that was completed for the designer's design class at Ball State University. The designer was given a hypothetical client (Berkshire Museum) and went out to take photogrecphs of a local building in order to create a wayfinding system through the use of Adobe CS. From personal research this system was developed based on what the designer believed the museum should display for simple user navigation. Signage is used within this environment to guide users to their desired location with minimal effort.

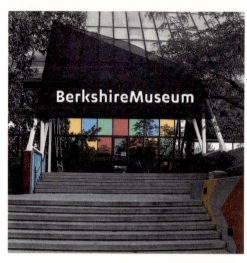

1 Aquarium ///// ///// Spark Lab
2 Innovation //// //// Mini World
3 A Part of Art /// //// Collections
4 Butterflies ///// Rocks & Minerals

DISCOVER

EXPLORE

Dive Deep With AQUARIUM CREATURES

A Look into the PERMANENT COLLECTION

I Am A PART OF ART

Wayfinding and Signage for a Rare Book Museum

Completion
2013
Designer
Edriel A. Collazo Beltrán
Location
Old San Juan, Puerto Rico
Photography
Edriel A. Collazo Beltrán

La Casa del Libro (rare book museum) is one of the world's best known archives for historical documents, particularly rare books and manuscripts. In this upcoming year the museum will be moved to new facilities. This project explores typographic systems and possibilities to add a graphic, textured communication platform to the museum's setting. The designer tried a graphic approach that serves for permanent wayfinding and signage while offering a flexible system for everyday activities.

Objective: This was a class project. The designer was used to being told what to do, but in this case, the professor asked him to look at the museum and identify areas where graphic design could help the institution.

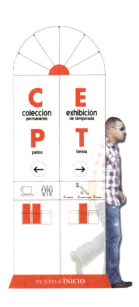

The designer aimed to provide visitors with a varied graphic language that would accompany, inform, visualise the space for them during a visit to the museum. In a way, he created a guide that does not speak to those who visit, but who talk to them in a visual manner, filling in gaps and pointing the way as one moves through the building. He intervened walls, floors and furniture, all with the hopes of altering unconventional areas to generate interest and points of focal attention. In a way, he wanted to turn the experience of moving through the museum into that of moving through a rare book.

The Pushkin State Museum of Fine Arts

Completion
2014

Design Agency
Just Design

Designers
Varya Mikhaylova,
Sergey Mongayt,
Denis Zolotarev

Client
The Pushkin State
Museum of Fine Arts

Location
Moscow, Russia

Photography
Natasha Polskaya

The Pushkin State Museum of Fine Arts is one of the most important art institutions in Moscow. Its Private Collections Department occupies an extremely complex historical building (actually, there are three formerly separate buildings), which displays some first-class permanent art collections as well as temporary shows. The wayfinding system was designed to be helpful, flexible, but not overbearing. It adjusts to ever-changing exhibition space and blends well into interior.

Выход Exit
Гардероб Cloakroom

 Аудитория Auditorium

Rio de Janeiro Wayfinding for FIFA World Cup 2014

Completion
2014

Client
Tátil Design

Design Agency
ICON

Location
Rio de Janeiro, Brazil

Designers
Luiz Mello, Gustavo Soares,
Ricardo Bacellar,
Silvia Araújo

Photography
Marcelo Coelho

Rio de Janeiro was one of the main cities for FIFA World Cup Brazil 2014 hosting seven matches, including the Final. The mobility plan developed by the City Authorities focused in routing people from major transportation nodes and areas of interest to the Maracanã Stadium via Metro and then back.

ICON defined a wayfinding strategy of route hierarchy developing two categories of signs. Firstly, educational sign, which was made up of a 5 sign-type family installed in the Metro system; these were intended to inform locals on the dates and times of matches and spectators on access and stations for the stadium itself. Secondly, wayfinding, a 13 sign-type family installed throughout the city that sat alongside with the look elements developed by the client.

ICON delivered 34 scope reports and more than 500 artworks that generated over 2,000 signs to aid the user experience for 14 metro stations, 1 train station, 4 rapid bus stations, 1 ferry station, 1 cruze terminal, 3 bus terminals, 2 airports and 15 walking routes. It is estimated that more than 885,000 people used this system.

London 2012 Olympics – Wayfinding and Temporary Signage

Completion
2012
Designers
Marcello Minale, Peter Brown
Client:
TfL (Transport for London)
Location
London, UK
Photography
in-house

Challenge:
The MinaleTattersfield London office was commissioned by Transport for London to design a dynamic and flexible signage system for the London 2012 Olympics. The area included Last Mile pedestrian routes for spectator travel from transport nodes (rail, bus, tube, etc.) to Olympic venues.

Solution:
Incorporating best practice from previous Olympic and Paralympic Games and other major sporting events, Minale Tattersfield set out the ground rules for a wayfinding strategy in the form of a Kit-of-Parts manual.

A variety of sign types were designed according to their use and location such as wall-and lamppost-mounted signs and distinctive information monoliths. The location of all Olympic signs and sign type was then set out across relevant routes.

Result:
The London 2012 Games was widely regarded as being one of the most successful ever in terms of organisation. The clarity of the signage system enabling visitors to get easily round the sites and public transport system played a large part in this.

London 2012 Olympic logo

London 2012 Paralympic logo

Olympic logo showing exclusion zone

Paralympic logo showing exclusion zone

Exclusion zone

Examples showing exclusion zones on angled spaces.

Single pictogram messages

Multi-pictogram messages

Facility pictogram messages

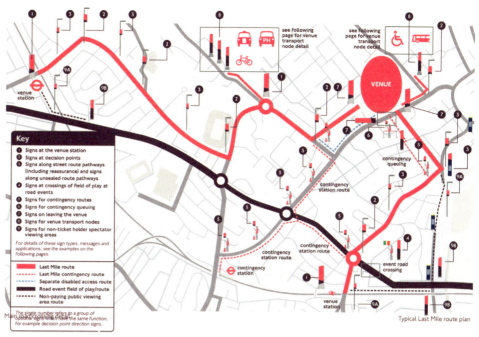

Main road crossing

Typical Last Mile route plan

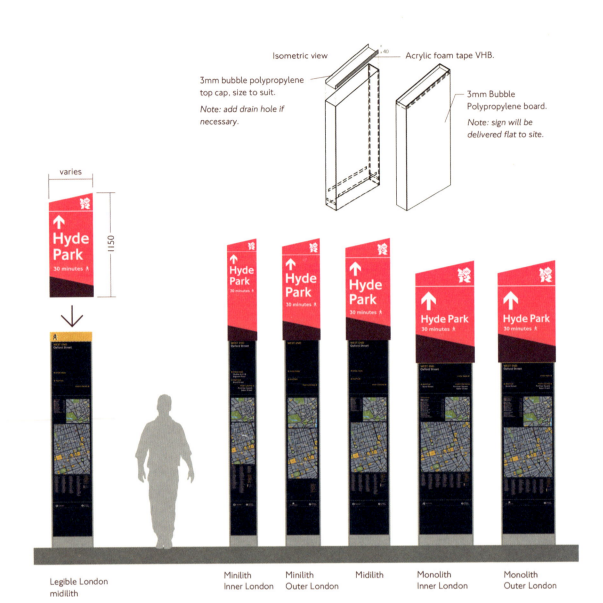

Isometric view

3mm bubble polypropylene top cap, size to suit.

Note: add drain hole if necessary.

Acrylic foam tape VHB.

3mm Bubble Polypropylene board.

Note: sign will be delivered flat to site.

varies

1150

Legible London midilith

Minilith Inner London

Minilith Outer London

Midilith

Monolith Inner London

Monolith Outer London

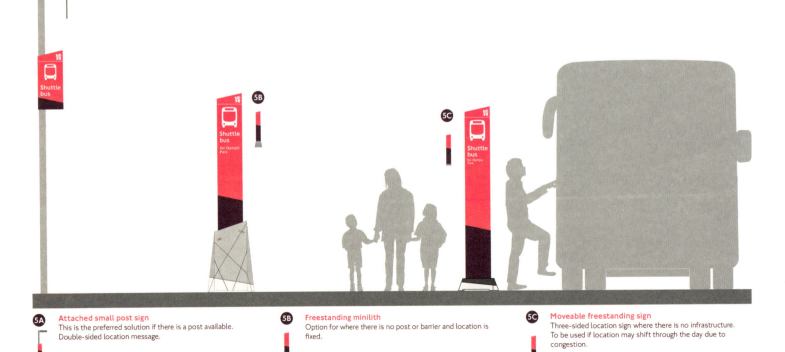

5A **Attached small post sign**
This is the preferred solution if there is a post available.
Double-sided location message.

5B **Freestanding minilith**
Option for where there is no post or barrier and location is fixed.

5C **Moveable freestanding sign**
Three-sided location sign where there is no infrastructure.
To be used if location may shift through the day due to congestion.

INDEX